Intertextuality in García Márquez

Intertextuality in García Márquez

Arnold M. Penuel

Spanish Literature Publications Company
York, South Carolina
1994

Library of Congress Catalog Card Number 93-84976

ISBN 0-938972-20-0

Printed in the United States of America

To the memory of my parents

Acknowledgments

I am most grateful to *Hispanic Journal* for permission to reprint, as Chapter 5, my article, "The Theme of Colonialism in García Márquez's 'La increíble y triste historia de la cándida Eréndira y de su abuela desalmada.'" 10 (Fall 1988): 67-83. As usual, Mrs. Bettye Leslie has typed the many revisions of the manuscript with patience and good cheer. I am sincerely grateful for her expert assistance. Also, I wish to express my appreciation to Centenary College for granting me the sabbatical leave that enabled me to complete this study.

Contents

For the novelist working in prose, the object is always entangled in someone else's discourse about it, it is already present with qualifications, an object of dispute that is conceptualized and evaluated variously, inseparable from the heteroglot social apperception of it.

Mikhail Bakhtin

Preface

The literary phenomenon now known as *intertextuality* most assuredly predates the ancient biblical insight that "there is nothing new under the sun." Yet, like most truths, this one must be considered partial and subject to numerous qualifications. It may even be considered as a hyperbole, expressing the notion that nothing is ever wholly new. If not taken literally, it does express a profound insight, one that is central to and ratified by the concept of intertextuality. Julia Kristeva coined the term in 1969, stating that "any text is constructed as a mosaic of quotations; any text is the absorption and transformation of another. The notion of *intertextuality* replaces that of intersubjectivity . . ." (*The Kristeva Reader* 37). Later, in *Revolution in Poetic Language*, she expressed a preference for the term *transposition* instead of intertextuality, though most theorists and critics continue to prefer her original term: ". . . [W]e prefer the term *transposition* because it specifies that the passage from one signifying system to another demands a new articulation of the thetic—of enunciative and denotative positionality" (60).

Broadly defined, intertextuality may be taken to include any pre-existing text (*intertext* or *pre-text*) adopted, adapted, and assimilated by a writer for his own purposes. This may include a writer's own texts, as well as those of other writers. Some critics go as far as to claim that "the notion of intertextuality opens all cultural facts and artefacts to the internal exchanges between them, or it opens up words to make them yield the 'infinite modalities' of language" (Parisier Plottel and Charney vii). Language itself, then, is a kind of intertextuality or pre-text, as are all the pre-existing resources, created by oneself or by others, whether known or anonymous, available for assimilation and reorganization in more or less original ways in presumably new circumstances. In practice, critics have assumed, for the most part, that intertextual studies encompass sources, influences, imitation, mythology, archetypes, allusions, words, ideas, plagiarism, self-plagiarism, and presuppositions. Since there is disagreement as to what exactly the term embraces, it is still in the process of being defined. Some critics exclude conscious allusions; others, like Jonathan Culler in *The Pursuit of Signs*, insist on "the intertextual nature of any verbal construct" (101).

Often, those who attempt to explain the term use the words "collage" or "palimpsest." Another integral part of the notion of intertextuality is *polyphony* (Bakhtin) or a multiplicity of voices. Each voice has its own value, but is also integrated into a larger whole and must be understood in the context of the surrounding voices. Intertextuality entails a dialogue among texts. A text is considered to be not so much about non-linguistic reality as it is a commentary on other texts. One of the tasks of intertextual studies is to make explicit a writer's presuppositions. Any writer, as Culler observes, winds up "postulating general expectations, implicit and explicit knowledge which will make his discourse intelligible . . ." (101). Although theorists and critics may disagree on the precise scope of intertextuality, there seems to be wide agreement that intertextual studies can be a means of both deconstructing and reconstructing a text.

It is evident, then, that intertextuality brings a broad cultural approach to the study of a text, postulating that any text is a reflection of one or more cultural traditions without, of course, denying the text's original elements, the possibility that it may transcend the culture of which it is a product. Intertextuality takes into account the Marxist emphasis on the historicity of the text without falling into a determinism that logically precludes originality. At the same time it avoids the textual solipsism of the New Criticism.

Kristeva's conception of intertextuality derives largely from the writings of Mikhail Bakhtin, especially from his study of carnivalized discourse in Rabelais, and his notion of *heteroglossia*, developed in his study of Dostoievsky and in *The Dialogic Imagination*. Bakhtin traces the origins of what he calls carnivalized discourse to the carnivals and fairs of medieval folk culture. Ultimately, it consists of a challenge to and a correction of the one-sided "official version" of reality presented by the "official culture" of Rabelais's time. In his brilliant analysis of

Rabelais's incorporation of this medieval tradition in *Gargantua and Pantagruel*, Bakhtin developed a coherent and compelling theory of the carnivalesque tradition or grotesque realism in literature. Moreover, he presents a history of the tradition, analyzing its diverse manifestations in literature since Rabelais's time. In *Problems of Dostoievsky's Poetics* and *The Dialogic Imagination* he expands his theory, which basically embraces two points of view or voices (polar oppositions), to elaborate a far-reaching and complex theory of the novel, according to which the language of this genre consists of multiple voices (*polyphony*) or types of discourse, and preeminence is given to context rather than to the text. This latter integrative condition he terms *heteroglossia*. Bakhtin contrasts novelists like Tolstoy, whose language he considers "monologic" and authoritarian, with that of writers like Dostoievsky, in whose fiction the reader hears many voices, many types of discourse, with no dogmatic or overbearing authorial voice attempting to preempt the reader's judgment by drowning out the other voices. The reader must listen to all the voices and sort out meanings for himself. Heteroglossia relativizes the textual meanings. Diverse types of discourse originate in diverse literary traditions and reflect diverse epochs, places, social classes, and professions. Moreover, they are subject to interpretations deriving from virtually inexhaustible contexts. Heteroglossia also entails the points of view of the author and the reader in its integrative process. The principal basis of the dialogue among texts, heteroglossia explains, as indicated above, why the subject matter of literature is not so much reality as it is other texts.

García Márquez's fiction presents an interesting challenge to intertextual studies. First, because the Colombian writer brings to his fiction a wide reading background, spanning the centuries from Homer's time down to the present. Second, because, like most great writers, he is quite adept at covering his authorial tracks. Although he has revealed the identity of many of his favorite writers through numerous interviews—especially in the lengthy conversations with Plinio Apuleyo Mendoza— the novelist is reserved about the writers who have influenced him, and, for the most part, he has spoken of influences only in a general way. Moreover, he invents and avails himself of an ample repertory of means to conceal his intertexts: displacement, the combination of displacement and straightforwardness, condensation, metaphor, juxtaposition, hyperbole, irony, paradox, and symbolism. Although his fiction can be read with pleasure on many levels, the stronger the reader's collaborative effort the richer the yield of meanings and the greater the pleasure. Needless to say, perhaps, a great part of this yield is produced in the discovery of the intertexts that lie hidden in his fiction.

Much has been written ferreting out and illuminating García Márquez's intertexts, but much remains to be done. The purpose of this study is to add to the growing intertextual understanding of his fiction. Although I include works from the various periods of his literary career, this is not meant to be a systematic study of his entire production nor is there an attempt to exhaust the intertexts of the texts studied. Indeed, such an effort would be in vain, inconsistent with the nature of intertextuality. The study focuses, rather, on certain intertexts that, notwithstanding their significance, have been overlooked or insufficiently explored by other critics. It is my hope that the study will not only be persuasive with regard to the intertexts discussed but that it will also ratify Culler's dictum "that one can often produce heat and light by rubbing two texts together" (118).

December 1992
Barrington, New Hampshire

Chapter 1

La casa de Bernarda Alba and *La mala hora*

Although there are significant differences between Lorca's *La casa de Bernarda Alba* (1936) and García Márquez's *La mala hora* (1962), the two works present striking similarities both in their general patterns and in certain details, suggesting that the Colombian novelist, consciously or unconsciously, was influenced by the Spanish poet and dramatist in the writing of this novel. The similarities manifest themselves in structure, themes, imagery, symbolism, and certain techniques or devices. Considering the kindred sensibilities and ideologies of the two writers, Lorca's influence on García Márquez should come as no surprise. Both writers reacted against the authoritarian morality and world-view of an ultraconservative Catholicism repressive of the instinctual life and individual freedom. In both works the writers avail themselves of a broad range of techniques to develop their themes in plastic and powerful ways. Both are masters at inventing imagery to create atmospheres replete with symbolic suggestion. Just how close these ideological and aesthetic affinities are will become evident in the analysis that follows.

Both *Bernarda Alba* and *La mala hora* are about the tyrannical and arbitrary exercise of power. Lorca's focus is primarily on the harmful impact on Bernarda's family of the exercise of such power, though scenes such as Prudencia's visit at the beginning of the third act attest to the pervasiveness of the problem in the town as a whole. Although Bernarda attempts to exercise total control over her household, she inflicts the most devastating harm on her daughters in her efforts to deny them any gratification of their sexual and maternal instincts. Her attempts to control the natural impulses of her daughters by virtually making them prisoners in their own home, under the guise of observing mourning for her recently deceased husband, creates an extremely frustrating and sterile life for all and eventually provokes a rebellion leading to tragedy. Appropriately enough, the tone of the play is tensely dramatic. Bernarda comes on strong from beginning to end, whereas the mayor of *La mala hora*, though increasingly firm in his control of the town, often uses indirect and underhanded methods to maintain control. Moreover, *La mala hora* has the relatively slower rhythm typical of the novel.

Against the background of *la violencia* in the Columbia of 1948-1962 *La mala hora* chronicles the tensions and conflicts leading to the disintegration of a town and culminating in civil war. Again, as in *Bernarda Alba*, the principal cause of the disintegration is the attempt by one individual (with the help of his associates) to exercise absolute control over the lives of others. This individual is a mayor who has been imposed (and imposes himself) on the town by the winners of the last round of what seems to be a never-ending violence. Although he physically imposes himself on the town with the aid of three deputies, who are known murderers, he is also aided by the priest Father Angel and Judge Arcadio. As the mayor discovers that he can become rich through his total "legal" control of the town what began as the exercise of power for power's sake gradually becomes an exercise of power for the sake of gain. As Angel Rama has pointed out, the connection between power and economic gain is quite close and deep-rooted in Latin America: "El poder político que se ejerce desde el alcalde, está vinculado estrechamente a un sustrato económico, tal como se le ve en *La mala hora*, estableciendo esa habitual conexión de las tierras americanas . . ." (37). But again, as in *Bernarda Alba*, the mayor's authoritarian methods culminate in rebellion with many of the townspeople disappearing into the mountains to take up arms against his tyranny. Both works explore the theme of the circularity of a repression provoking a rebellion which in turn leads to stronger efforts of repression. In this regard, Felicia Hardison Londré is certainly on target in her perception of *Bernarda Alba's* circular structure:

> Some critics suggest that Bernarda's authority
> within the house will permanently be improved by
> Adela's rebellion, while others, more plausibly, given
> the play's deliberate circular construction, see that the

tragedy is not only the death of Adela but also the fact
that her death will change nothing (179).[1]

The theme of acquisitiveness is clearly present in the play,
but of secondary importance. It is evident to all the characters, as
well as to the reader, that Pepe el Romano intends to marry the
withered Angustias for the money she has inherited. Also, privilege and class feelings are in evidence in the conversations between Poncia and the other servant and between Poncia and
Bernarda. In *La mala hora* the use of arbitrary power for the un-
ethical acquisition of other's property is a principal object of criticism.

Class tensions constitute an important theme in both
works. Most of the lampoons in *La mala hora* are posted at the
expense of the rich and powerful whose wealth has been acquired, as in the mayor's case, through theft and the abuse of
power, mutually sanctioned by members of the ruling clique.
For this reason the appearance of the lampoons is a source of anticipation and pleasure for the poor in the town: "Aquella tarde,
el padre Angel observó que también en la casa de los pobres se
hablaba de los pasquines, pero de un modo diferente y hasta con
una saludable alegría" (104).

In *Bernarda Alba* Lorca does not focus directly on the exploitation of the poor by the rich but rather on a strong and pervasive class feeling that could certainly be a condition for and a
consequence of such exploitation. As the following exchange
indicates, Bernarda, more than anyone else, exemplifies this attitude:

BERNARDA
Los pobres son como los animales; parece como si es-
tuvieran hechos de otras sustancias.

MUJER 1.ª
Los pobres sienten también sus penas.

BERNARDA
Pero las olvidan delante de un plato de garbanzos (18).

Consider also that Bernarda had driven away Enrique Humanas,
a suitor of Martirio's, because his father was a farm laborer (82).
The theme of class tensions also emerges early in the play in the
conversation between Poncia and the other servant, revealing
Poncia's hatred of Bernarda. Speaking of the daughters' posses-

sions, the servant exclaims "¡Ya quisiera tener yo lo que ellas!"
Poncia replies: "Nosotras tenemos nuestras manos y un hoyo en
la tierra de la verdad" (15).

The lampoons in *La mala hora* are not only seen in different lights by the novel's various characters but also reveal a variety of symbolic implications, depending on the analytical focus.
From one perspective they are, as Señor Benjamín says, "un
síntoma de descomposición social" (122). Their clandestine nature and their exposure of supposedly known but nonetheless
unsavory facts about the town's elite is certainly symptomatic of
social disintegration. Moreover, the action suggested by Father
Angel and the measures actually taken to suppress the lampoons
by the mayor precipitate the town's definitive disintegration.
Thinking of the lampoons and seeking a remedy for a headache,
Judge Arcadio exclaims to Dr. Giraldo: "Todo el pueblo tiene do-
lor de cabeza" (28). The town suffers from the same atmosphere
of ill will, rancor, and envy that afflicts Bernarda Alba's house
and town. The most recent lampoon, Arcadio learns, is about
Raquel Contreras: ". . . [Q]ue los viajes que ha hecho este año no
fueron para calzarse los dientes, como ella dice, sino para abor-
tar" (29). Similarly, in *Bernarda Alba*, in addition to the endless
tensions in Bernarda's own house, we witness Bernarda's and
the other townspeople pitiless treatment of the unmarried
daughter of Librada when the body of her dead child is discovered. Bernarda and others clamor for her death before the
authorities arrive: "¡Matadla! ¡Matadla!" (91). Bernarda's conversation with Prudencia further illustrates the poisoned atmosphere of the town. Prudencia's husband avoids his brothers
after he has quarrelled with them over an inheritance. He has
also quarrelled with a supposedly disobedient daughter and refuses to forgive her (92-93). Bernarda, of course, totally approves
of what she considers the manly attitude Prudencia's husband
has assumed in these matters: "Es un verdadero hombre" (93).
Referring to Prudencia's daughter, she remarks: "Una hija que
desobedece deja de ser hija para convertirse en una enemiga"
(93). In passing, it should be noted that Bernarda's comments on
these situations betray her will to total control of her daughters'
actions. She locks up her demented mother María Josefa out of
fear of what the neighbors would say should they see or hear
her. Of the similarity in the techniques the two writers use to re-
inforce the oppressive atmosphere of their respective novelistic
towns I will say more later.

In order to exercise total control over her daughters' actions Bernarda exaggerates the custom of mourning, turning her home into a virtual prison. Early in the play she announces the severity and length of the observance, which is tantamount to placing her daughters under house arrest: "En ocho años que dure el luto no ha de entrar en esta casa el viento de la calle. Hacemos cuenta que hemos tapiado con ladrillos puertas y ventanas. Así pasó en casa de mi padre y en casa de mi abuelo" (25).[2] Poncia offers another perspective, calling the house a convent (66). Angustias exults in the prospect of leaving "este infierno" (51). In the last act, when Adela openly rebels against Bernarda, she exclaims: "¡Aquí se acabaron las voces de presidio!" (120). Then, there is the prison within the prison: the solitary confinement of María Josefa, whose madness requires that she be kept out of sight and earshot. Reed Anderson cogently argues that the confinement "that structures the consciousness of the characters" is a "metaphor of oppression and the enslavement of the spirit and the will to the uncompromising authority of inherited values" (121).

What Bernarda tries to accomplish through the custom of mourning, the mayor seeks to accomplish with the civil custom of the curfew. The attempts fail in both cases, ultimately contributing to the rebellion of those they seek to control. The mayor arrests, tortures, and finally murders Pepe Amador, the hapless young man caught distributing clandestine political leaflets. Amador is a scapegoat; the mayor knows, notwithstanding his affirmations to the contrary, that Amador is not the author of the lampoons. Just as the mayor's efforts to suppress the lampoons are ineffectual so are Father Angel's efforts to dictate the standards of morality in the community. Despite his efforts to censure what he considers immoral movies, he is not always successful; and he utterly fails to persuade Arcadio's common-law wife to legalize their relations through marriage (80-81). Nor is he able to curb the illicit but exuberant and largely healthy sexual activities of the townspeople (27, 34). As Dulce Andrigueto has pointed out (26-27), Father Angel's efforts to suppress the instinctual life of his parishioners is no more effective than his efforts to eliminate the mice that proliferate in his church.[3] The priest's preoccupations are not only petty, futile, and archaic, but they are also ultimately counterproductive. Pressured by Asis's widow to preach against the lampoons (97), the priest fails to summon the courage and the words to do so

(156). Instead, he admonishes the mayor to take measures to end the appearance of the lampoons (127-30). The mayor's solution is to impose a curfew on the town, which is equivalent to placing all the citizens of the town under house arrest from dark until dawn. Father Angel describes the lampoons as "un caso de terrorismo en el orden moral" (130), which ironically is more applicable to his own efforts to censorship and refusal to extend communion to women who appear at mass in short sleeves (106). Again, as occurs in *Bernarda Alba* with Bernarda's household, the priest attempts to hold the town hostage to his archaic moral values.

The efforts of censorship and political control which in *La mala hora* are the work of the mayor, the priest, and indirectly the town's prominent citizens, in *Bernarda Alba* are the work of Bernarda herself, though it is clear that her values are also the town's dominant values. Bernarda's tactics range from verbal abuse and intimidation to the use of physical force and even include, as indicated above, the confinement of her mother in a locked room. Bernarda's first and last words in the play are "¡Silencio!" (18, 122), revealing both her will-to-power and the sterility of her purit[yr]an[n]ical morality. When Bernarda learns from Poncia that the 39-year-old Angustias has been trying to observe and listen to the men who are present at the wake, she must be restrained by Foncia. Later, she again resorts to physical violence after she discovers that Martirio took Angustias's photograph of Pepe. This time Angustias intervenes to restrain her mother. From beginning to end the play is replete with examples of Bernarda's pathological need to control everyone around her. Anyone who has read the play can think of numerous such instances. That she is not just domineering but aggressively and pathologically domineering is evident in the following speech addressed to her daughters: "No os hagáis ilusiones de que vais a poder conmigo. ¡Hasta que salga de esta casa con los pies adelante mandaré en lo mío y en lo vuestro!" (47). What begins for the mayor as a more or less automatic exercise of authority, under the guise of maintaining "el principio de la autoridad" (142), eventually becomes a means of acquiring land.

Although the lampoons mean different things to different characters, embarrassment to the rich and powerful (75), moral terrorism to Father Angel (130), a source of novelty and suspense to most, a cause for happiness to the poor (104), and a threat to authority for the mayor, after all is said and done, they are, as

Señor Benjamín perceives, "un síntoma de descomposición social" (122). The lampoons symbolize the weak but persistent voice of truth which when it cannot be voiced openly seeks alternative means of expression. Competing with the passion of acquisitiveness, lust for power, sexuality, and puritanism, the truth is almost elbowed out of the way. Its relative weakness notwithstanding, it is the persistent expression of the truth that leads to the open rebellion against the mayor and his associates. It is not so much the content of the lampoons that matters, since most of what is said is already public knowledge (75), but rather the persistence of the will to defy the powers that be. Still, the objectification of what is already known is of consequence in that it constitutes publicly shared confirmation of certain injustices around which the townspeople can galvanize their rebellious energies. Psychologically, the irrepressibility of the lampoons is a tribute to the townspeople's resilience, and ultimately presupposes a positive, hopeful view of human nature on the "implied author's" part. Just as the gimmick in *El coronel no tiene quien le escriba* is a symbol of vitality and resistance, so are the lampoons in *La mala hora*. Truth and freedom may be temporarily suppressed, but even in the worst circumstances there is an often faint but nonetheless persistent force in human nature that resists and seeks to overcome such suppression. With his materialism and lust for power, the mayor is blind to this side of human nature. In his view, fear and greed are the principal if not the sole levers for controlling human conduct.

Although it is natural that the lampoons should be posted under the cover of darkness, it is also symbolically appropriate that their origins, which are rooted deep in human nature, should remain invisible, especially to the mayor and Father Angel. This also clarifies why Casandra tells the mayor that "es todo el pueblo y no es nadie" (149). This assertion can be interpreted to mean that it is an expression of the town's collective will, but it is also a cogent psychological insight on Casandra's part: this is the townspeople's way of reacting to oppressive conditions. Paradoxically, the act of rebellion which from one perspective signifies the disintegration of authority in the town, from another perspective signifies a healthy effort by the townspeople to recover their dignity as human beings.

What García Márquez achieves in *La mala hora* with the original device of the lampoons, Lorca achieves in *Bernarda Alba* with a variety of means. The conversation at the beginning of the play between Poncia and the other servant provides the reader/spectator an early insight into Bernarda's personality, revealing at the same time Poncia's intense hatred of the domineering widow. María Josefa's insanity suggests many ramifications, but one of her most important symbolic functions is to voice the discontentment felt by the daughters, as well as their longings to satisfy their sexual and maternal instincts in a normal fashion. Her status as a madwoman allows her to express these truths without Bernarda taking the content seriously, though for fear of gossip she does lock her mother out of sight. When María Josefa escapes from her room at the beginning of Act I, she refuses to obey Bernarda, who has told her to be quiet:

> No, no me callo. No quiero ver a estas mujeres solteras rabiando por la boda, haciéndose polvo el corazón, y yo me quiero ir a mi pueblo. Bernarda, yo quiero un varón para casarme y para tener alegría (48).

In her singsong utterances toward the end of Act III, María Josefa's censure of her tyrannical daughter is a type of lampoon:

> Bernarda,
> cara de leoparda.
> Magdalena,
> cara de hiena.
> ¡Ovejita!
> Meee, meee.
> Vamos a los ramos del portal de Belén (112, see also 113-14).

As in *La mala hora*, the characters in *Bernarda Alba* also reveal their discontentment and longings through their conversations with each other and through the growing tensions these conversations disclose. Increasingly, Bernarda's daughters no longer see each other as sisters, but as rivals. Feeling compassion for the hapless Martirio, Adela impulsively tries to console her by embracing her. But her jealous sister full of hatred rejects her embrace: "¡No me abraces! No quieras ablandar mis ojos. Mi sangre ya no es la tuya, aunque quisiera verte como hermana, no te miro ya más que como mujer" (117). Adela's surreptitious rebellion, which, like the posting of the lampoons, takes place at night, culminates, as in *La mala hora*, in open rebellion when she is confronted by Bernarda after a rendezvous with Pepe el Romano:

ADELA
(Haciéndole frente)
¡Aquí se acabaron las voces de presidio! (ADELA
arrebata un bastón a su madre y lo parte en dos.) Esto
hago yo con la vara de la dominadora. No dé un paso
más. En mí no manda nadie más que Pepe (120).[4]

Just as the rebellion initiated with the lampoons in *La mala hora*
is a healthy act of self-affirmation, so is Adela's rebellion, though
it ends tragically, an act of healthy self-affirmation. In both
works the abuse of power, which makes human fulfillment and
autonomy difficult, if not impossible, leaves rebellion and violence as the only solutions. *La mala hora* reveals how the
violence is perpetuated in a never-ending circle of provocation
and reaction. In *Bernarda Alba*, Bernarda's reaction to Adela's
rebellion and death makes it clear that she has learned nothing.
Her reaction is to tighten her grip on her daughters' conduct.

Vargas Llosa was the first to point out the importance of
the unreal or imaginary in *La mala hora*, convincingly arguing
that the movement from the plane of objective reality to what
he calls the plane of the unreal or imaginary is subtle and gradual (423-36; see also Lydia D. Hazera 480-81).[5] Ultimately, says
Vargas Llosa in *Historia de un deicidio*, reality gives way to the
imaginary: "[L]o imaginario acaba por derrotar a lo real ob-
jetivo . . ." (426). As partial evidence, he cites the widow of
Montiel's retreat to "lo imaginario gracias a una locura cierta o
fingida" (423) which "por afinidad esencial" enables her to
identify the nature of the lampoons before anyone else (450).
Mina's blind grandmother, who makes dire predictions of a
coming catastrophe, further evidences the movement toward an
imaginary reality. She announces to Father Angel that "la
sangre correrá por las calles y no habrá poder humano capaz de
detenerla" (165). Her function here parallels that of the demented but prophetic María Josefa in *Bernarda Alba* who, speaking of Bernarda's daughters, exclaims that Pepe el Romano "os
va a devorar porque vosotras sois granos de trigo" (114).

Deluding himself, the mayor is reluctant to give much
importance to the lampoons, telling Arcadio that "la gente está
feliz" (141). Later, the judge's observation about the nature of
the town provides additional evidence of the sway of *lo imaginario* in the town: "Este es un pueblo fantasma" (172).

The lampoons are the product of a subtle sphere of human nature where truth and freedom are valued, a sphere

which, as indicated above, is invisible to the mayor, who believes that physical force, fear, and greed are the levers for controlling the town. Referring to the mayor's helplessness with regard to the lampoons, Vargas Llosa perceptively notes the mayor's incapacity to comprehend inner human realities: "El teniente es todopoderoso en la realidad objetiva, pero está indefenso contra ellos [the lampoons], porque no proceden de esa misma realidad" (453).

The failure to understand the psychology underlying the appearance of the lampoons conditions the mayor's imposition of the curfew and leads him to arrest, torture, and murder Pepe Amador, both precipitating causes of the townspeople's recourse to open rebellion. In the final pages, it is clear that the mayor continues to try to impose his reality on a larger reality he fails to understand when, referring to Pepe Amador, he emphatically warns his henchmen that "este muchacho no ha muerto" (197). Writing of the importance of psychology in the novel, Hazera has acutely observed: "Lo psicológico actúa como una carga subterránea que fluye y refluye con gran fuerza para imponer al realismo minucioso de la obra el elemento subjetivo que le da su mayor hilación y coherencia" (473).

Bernarda Alba's efforts to impose her will (her subjective reality) on objective reality are in evidence from her first appearance in the play until the end. Although two other characters, including her own daughter Angustias, saw Pepe el Romano at the wake, Bernarda insists that he was not present: "Estaba su madre. Ella ha visto a su madre. A Pepe no lo ha visto ella ni yo" (20). Apparently, Bernarda is unwilling to admit that she or her daughters are capable of noticing the presence of any man. Bernarda also deceives herself with regard to her motivation for removing her daughters from any contact with men and the outside world. A remark made by Poncia reinforces the play's ubiquitous evidence of Bernarda's repressed sexuality. Women attending mass, says Bernarda, should take no notice of the men present: "La mujeres no deben de mirar más hombre que al oficiante, y ése porque tiene faldas. Volver la cabeza es buscar el calor de la pana" (21). Poncia murmurs perceptively: "¡Sarmentosa por calentura de varon!" (21).

Like the mayor, Bernarda is blind to the invisible world of the human need for freedom and truth. When she refuses to perceive the real significance of Martirio's theft of the photograph of Pepe, Poncia tells her: "Ahora estás ciega" (81). As tensions grow, Bernarda, always more concerned with appearances than with reality, insists on accepting at face value Martirio's excuse that she took the photo as a joke. She refuses to listen to Angustias' complaint that Martirio does not love her: "Cada uno sabe lo que piensa por dentro. Yo no me meto en los corazones, pero quiero buena fachada y armonía familiar. ¿Lo entiendes?" (100). Here the ability to attain an objective understanding of human nature on the deepest levels seems to be incompatible with the effort to control others' conduct. Speaking of Lorca's literary production as a whole, Francisco Ruiz Ramón makes an observation that is certainly applicable to *Bernarda Alba*:

> El universo dramático de Lorca, como totalidad y en cada una de sus piezas, está estructurado sobre una sola situación básica, resultante del enfrentamiento conflictivo de dos series de fuerzas que, por reducción a su esencia, podemos designar *principio de autoridad y principio de libertad* (177).

Perhaps this same opposition of forces produces the tensions of *La mala hora*.

At the end of Act III, when Bernarda and Martirio give Adela to understand that Pepe el Romano has been killed, Bernarda, again motivated by the desire to maintain appearances and against the background of a perverse ideology, attempts to impose her will on objective reality: "¡Mi hija ha muerto virgen! ¡Nadie diga nada! Ella ha muerto virgen" (123). The play then ends with these self-deluding words: "Ella, la hija menor de Bernarda Alba, ha muerto virgen. ¿Me habéis oído? ¡Silencio, silencio he dicho! ¡Silencio!" (123). Two situations certainly display astonishing similarities, and suggest that, consciously or unconsciously, García Márquez was influenced by this passage in the mayor's warning to his henchmen that Pepe Amador had not died (197).[6]

In an interview with Plinio Apuleyo Mendoza, García Márquez, speaking of the mayor (as well as characters in other novels), explains his motivation in this way: "Power is a substitute for love" (108). He then adds: "The way I see it is that the inability to love is what drives them to seek consolation in power" (109). In my view, this insight also applies to Bernarda. Neither Bernarda nor the mayor consider their charges as ends-in-themselves, but rather seek to control their conduct for their own purposes. Knowledge used for self-aggrandizement and manipulative purposes seems to be at variance with the kind of understanding that accompanies love. As I have indicated above, Bernarda and the mayor are blind to the deepest needs of others, and by (psycho)logical extension, to their own deepest needs, albeit this is clearer in Bernarda's case then in that of the mayor.

The Church has a hidden, almost invisible role in *Bernarda Alba*. Lorca's focus is on the harm caused by Bernarda's pathological personality. It is clear that her inordinate need to dominate all those around her derives at least in part from her own sexual frustration and the town's regnant double standard for men and women in virtually all spheres of conduct, as well as the sexual. It is just as clear that Bernarda's puritanical sexual morality is shared by her fellow townspeople, as the scene involving Librada's daughter reveals. It is also clear that this puritanical asexual morality derives from the teachings of the Church. *Bernarda Alba* explores and illuminates the lives of those subjected to such a narrow, ill-conceived morality. For this reason, the play ends with Bernarda's insistence that her daughter has died a virgin. True, Bernarda is a pathological case, but her extraordinary strength of will makes her an excellent instrument for dramatizing in a *reductio ad absurdum* the destructive consequences of a morality centered on instinctual renunciation. The Church is the *autor intelectual*, to use the Spanish phrase, of the crimes committed by Bernarda. This is the significance of the negative focus placed on the ringing of the church bells in the first words spoken in the play. The maid complains: "Ya tengo el doble de esas campanas metido entre las sienes" (11).

The play does present more positive, healthful modes of life: the songs of the reapers going to and coming from work (68-69), María Josefa's exaggerated but symbolically sound vision of what life should be (112-14). The Adela who has found love with Pepe el Romano displays a largeness of spirit hitherto absent in the play. When Bernarda and the townspeople are clamoring for the death by stoning of Librada's daughter, Adela, partly because she could suffer a similar fate, but partly out of a generosity born of fulfillment, is the only character who protests against this primitive urge to kill, which is ultimately based on resentment and envy (91). Later, this same psychology of fulfillment permits Adela to feel the empathy that leads her to attempt to embrace and console the frustrated Martirio (117).

Conversely, Martirio's lack of fulfillment leads her to reject Adela's generous gesture.

In *La mala hora*, through Father Angel, the Church plays a highly visible role. Although the priest shares Bernarda's narrow morality, as attested to by his constant efforts to censure movies and his attempt to persuade the judge and his pregnant common-law wife to marry, unlike Bernarda, Father Angel does not possess a pathological personality. On the contrary, as his name suggests, he is basically kind and well-intentioned, albeit ingenuous and shortsighted. His innocence, which in his case is a form of intellectual superficiality, not only leads him to attempt to control the sexual morality of the townspeople, but also leads him to admonish the mayor to take action to suppress the lampoons: "Lo he molestado—dijo el párroco, yendo directamente as sus propósitos—para manifestarle mi preocupación por su indiferencia ante los pasquines" (127). This occurs after the good Father fails to summon the courage to preach against the lampoons. In any case, Father Angel's advice to the mayor leads him to impose a curfew on the town. This drastic restriction convinces the townspeople that politically nothing has changed, setting the stage for their uprising. The priest's naïveté notwithstanding, it is clear, as Stephen Minta says, where his sympathies lie: "So we can see that Father Angel's natural allies in town are the influential, the powerful, and the conservative, and this, I think, accounts for his behavior in the matter of the lampoons" (87). Robert Kirsner is right in stressing the negative consequences of Father Angel's innocence: "And here the good priest, whose name is virtually allegorical, remains insensitive to the horror around him. He had benignly sought to ignore the pasquinades for fear of dignifying them and he merely succeeded in remaining aloof from the inner strife that surrounded him" (72). Another critic, Wolfgang A. Luchting points out the inadequacy of Father Angel's ideas: " . . . [T]he priest's terminology and the ideology it reveals are no longer relevant: social unrest and rebellion against social injustice can no longer be waved aside as 'sin'" (101). In my view, Father Angel, like the Church he represents, for a variety of reasons, but originating largely from his mirroring of the Church's intellectual poverty, suffers from a lack of good judgment. Concerned with what some ethicists term "microethical" matters such as the censorship of movies and adultery, he remains, as Luchting says, insensitive to the larger matters of social and political injustice. Although the mice are a polyvalent symbol, one symbolic implication of Father Angel's obsession with them is the smallness of his moral concerns. To some extent, Father Angel exemplifies what Hannah Arendt, writing of Adolph Eichmann, called the "banality of evil" (*passim*).

If in *Bernarda Alba* pathology and puritanical morality prove to be a fatal combination, in *La mala hora* naïveté and puritanical morality prove just as fatal. The common denominator in these two combinations is the puritanical morality of ultra-conservative Catholicism.

La mala hora also juxtaposes healthier attitudes with regard to human needs with the puritanical perspective represented by Father Angel. Judge Arcadio and his pregnant common-law wife are described waking up completely naked after having made love three times during the night. When Arcadio tactfully rejects his "wife's" sexual play, "ella soltó una risa cargada de buena salud" (27). When they notice the door of their house was wide open during their sexual play, they simply laugh (27-28). When Father Angel attempts to persuade Arcadio's wife to marry, she refuses, saying that others do what she does but under cover of darkness. Responding to Father Angel's insistence that she avoid becoming a victim of gossip, she points out that, unlike the "decent" women of the town, she has not been lampooned: "No tengo que ponerme a salvo de nada porque hago mis cosas a la luz del día. La prueba es que nadie se gasta su tiempo poniéndome un pasquín, y en cambio a todos los decentes de la plaza los tienen empapelados" (81).

Among the most striking parallels between the two works are those having to do with the writers' creation of imagery and atmosphere to create an atmosphere of fear and oppression.[7] Both writers rely heavily, but not exclusively, on climatic imagery. Throughout *Bernarda Alba* there are frequent complaints of oppressive heat. As Barry E. Weingarten has noted, "heat is an important leitmotiv" symbolizing the town's repressive sexual and moral atmosphere (134). Shortly after Bernarda returns from her husband's funeral, the following exchange takes place in her house:

MUJER 3.ª
Cae el sol como plomo

MUJER 1.ª
Hace años no he conocido calor igual
(Pausa. Se abanican todas.) (19).

Martirio complains of the heat and longs for the summer to end: "Estoy deseando que llegue noviembre, los días de lluvias, la escarcha, todo lo que no sea este verano interminable" (70). Not surprisingly, the heat eventually produces storms. Referring to the disappearance of Angustias's photograph of Pepe, Bernarda exclaims: "Ya veía la tormenta venir, pero no creía que estallara tan pronto" (78). Shortly before Adela is discovered returning from her rendezvous with Pepe, Poncia says to the other servant: "¡Tú ves este silencio? Pues hay una tormenta en cada cuarto. El día que estallen nos barrerán a todos" (109).

The situation of the enclosed stallion that kicks the wall during Prudencia's visit is similar to that of Bernarda's daughters. Like the daughters, who see and hear the reapers going to and coming from work, the stallion senses the close presence of the mares that are in heat. The explanation Bernarda gives in a low voice that he must be hot, reinforces the association between the heat and the town's sexually frustrating atmosphere.

The tempo of the appearance of natural images quickens early in Act III, foreshadowing the play's outcome. In general, the strong presence of external nature symbolizes the strong presence of nature within each of the characters. Having established the sexual significance of the stallion's restlessness early in Act III, the playwright exploits the original image for further symbolism. Following several remarks on the unusual darkness of the night, Adela comments on the size of the stallion: "El caballo garañón estaba en el centro del corral ¡blanco! Doble de grande, llenando todo lo oscuro" (102). Even the stars seem larger in the darkness of this night. Adela observes: "Tiene el cielo unas estrellas como puños" (102).

Specifically foreshadowing the revelation of Adela's rebellion are the comments made about shooting stars. Bernarda, Martirio, and Amelia do not like to see or think about shooting stars. Adela, on the other hand, is enthralled by the spectacle: "A mí me gusta ver correr lleno de lumbre lo que está quieto años enteros" (104). While her mother and sisters fear their passions, Adela, liberated from such fear, exults in hers. As indicated above, the night is a vague symbol in both works, under cover of which rebellion takes place. The night also symbolizes the dark, deep, and mysterious origins of human passions, which Bernarda and the mayor fail to see, understand, and accept.

Discussing the Colombian violence that took place around the middle of the century, George R. McMurray reports the novelists' view on his approach to the theme in *La mala hora*: "According to García Márquez, the principal defect of the Colombian novelists of *la violenca* is their propensity to describe the brutalities of the conflict directly instead of the ambiance of terror it produced" (21n). In *La mala hora*, then, García Márquez avails himself of the same type of symbolic language used earlier by Lorca in *Bernarda Alba* to present another type of violence. Both writers privilege a language that suggests and hints, reinforcing their themes unobtrusively and with subtlety.

La mala hora displays a wide array of imagery and other devices to create an ambiance reinforcing the novels' themes and leitmotivs. Like Lorca, García Márquez relies heavily on climatic imagery, especially rain and heat, but images of decay, beginning with that of the mayor's abscessed tooth, also abound in the novel. The lampoons themselves, a most original device, have a certain equivalence, as pointed out above, to devices used by Lorca. Although they have symbolic implications, they are not images per se. Father Angel's obsessive efforts to exterminate the mice parallel the mayor's attempt to suppress the lampoons. Among other implications, both the lampoons and the mice symbolize the persistence of the quest for freedom, truth, and the satisfaction of basic human needs, especially, but not exclusively, the satisfaction of sexual needs. They also illustrate how any religion or government that ignores such needs will ultimately be undermined in one way or another.

The dominant climatological image in *La mala hora* is rain. The novel's action takes place in October, the country's rainy season, and could be considered simply a realist device, but the rain is mentioned too often in contexts strengthening the impression of an oppressive political, social, and religious environment to be interpreted in this manner. The rain is an almost constant presence, being mentioned sometimes on several pages in succession. The references to rain are especially frequent at the beginning of the novel. César Montero's wife registers her feelings about the rain as her husband gets dressed early one morning: "Todavía está lloviendo—dijo ella, sintiendo que sus huesos adolescentes habían absorbido la humedad de la noche—. Me siento como una esponja" (11; see also 7, 8, 11, 12, 13, 19, 21, 23, 25). Later, the narrator twice uses the word *tregua* (50, 55) to refer to a lull in the rain, suggesting a state of siege in the town reflective of the political situation. Even when the rain stops, the threat remains, both in the form of floods and more rain.

The barber, who certainly harbors rebellious sentiments, "se extasió en el río turbio y amenazante. Había dejado de llover, pero una nube cargada se mantenía inmóvil sobre el pueblo (54; see also, 51, 99, 109, 117, 120, 122, 123, 124, 126, 144, 146, 147, 148, 150, 152, 153, 154, 159, 160, 186-87). The rain imagery also suggests the violence and constant threat of violence hanging over the townspeople's heads.

Along with the rain imagery, albeit not as frequent, are images having to do with heat, contributing to the ambiance of oppression in the novel. There is an abundance of such images: "el calor se hizo más intenso con la proximidad del mediodía (32), "se ahogaba en el caluroso dormitorio" (34), "si no abres la ventana nos vamos a morir de calor" (47), "la temperatura se hizo intolerable" (138-39), "esta casa está ardiendo" (140), "Atormentado por la fatiga de la vigilia y el calor" (167), "el aire se había vuelto seco y la casa estaba paralizada por el calor" (178), "nunca había hecho tanto calor en octubre" (178). Occasionally, rain and heat are combined in a single oppressive image, as a character complains: "Aunque llueva sigue haciendo calor" (120). When Father Angel denies the movie owner permission to show a movie because of Pastor's death, the businessman, vexed both by the unbearable heat and the oppressive moral climate, bitterly exclaims: "Esto es un infierno" (26).

Another dominant type of imagery in *La mala hora* is that of corruption and decay. The smell of dead mice in the church, the mayor's abscessed tooth (61-70), which, as Hazera has suggested, symbolizes the mayor's greed and corruption (474),[8] the dead cow caught on the river bank (88-89), the dead cat Father Angel sees floating among the flowers (59), and the vultures in the streets and other places (80, 119), all symbolize the corruption and disintegration of the town. The smells of corruption and decay are pervasive and unavoidable. The smell of the dead cow reaches the innermost recesses of the houses: "El tufo de la podredumbre permenció un momento sobre el muelle, se meció en la brisa matinal y entró hasta el fondo de las casas" (88). Hard on the heels of the mayor's scheming with Arcadio to have the town indemnify the former for the land on which the flood victims have settled, we find this passage comparing men with vultures:

> El señor Benjamín cambió el pie en la plataforma
> sin retirar la vista de los gallinazos que se disputaban
> una tripa en la mitad de la calle. Observó los

> movimientos difíciles de los animales engolados y cer-
> emoniosos como bailando una danza antigua, y admiró
> la fidelidad representativa de los hombres que se dis-
> frazan de gallinazos el domingo de quincuagésima
> (119).

The juxtaposition of this passage with the mayor's scheming (his ceremonious legal manipulations in the service of the "ancient dance" of greed) constitutes a clear characterization of the mayor and his associates.

Two incidents related at the beginning of Chapter Six are strongly reminiscent of the stallion scene in *Bernarda Alba*. Chapter Six presents what threatens from the beginning to be a difficult day for Father Angel, notwithstanding Trinidad's good news that she has caught six mice during the night. This chapter reveals growing tensions, culminating (in the following chapter) in the good priest's decision to express his concern to the mayor over his indifference to the threat of the lampoons. The first incident involves a burro: "un burro sin sueño se protegió de la lluvia bajo el alero de la casa cural, y estuvo toda la noche dando coces contra la pared del dormitorio. Fue una noche sin sosiego" (109). A few lines later, we read: "Aquella mañana Trinidad había encontrado un ratón enloquecido golpeándose contra las paredes después de haber buscado toda la noche la puerta de su casa" (110). In *Bernarda Alba* we find almost the same words to describe a similar situation; Bernarda explains to Prudencia that the blows she hears come from "el caballo garañón, que está encerrado y *da coces contra el muro* (94), (emphasis added). García Márquez has taken a single incident in *Bernarda Alba* and divided it into two incidents in *La mala hora*, symbolizing in this way the effects of oppression. The frustrated burro kicks the wall while the mouse goes crazy seeking a way out.

In the sections of Plinio Apuleyo Mendoza's interview with García Márquez in which the novelist talks about writers he has read and been influenced by, there is no mention of Lorca (39-52). Whether this is due to an oversight or the "anxiety of influence" is not clear. It is highly unlikely, however, that García Márquez was not thoroughly familiar at the time he wrote *La mala hora* with what is probably Lorca's most widely-read and widely-staged play. The ideological, thematic, esthetic, and structural affinities between the two works, as well as the close similarities in certain incidents suggest that, consciously or unconsciously, García Márquez was influenced by the popular

Spanish dramatist and poet in writing *La mala hora*. In saying this I am far from suggesting that the Colombian writer slavishly imitated the Spanish model. On the contrary, he simply found it convenient to avail himself of a similar aesthetic to explore similar themes in different circumstances, expanding the themes, adapting Lorca's aesthetic to his own purposes, while creating highly original devices, such as the lampoons, the mice, and the mayor's toothache to write a highly original and impressive novel.

Notes

[1] For a different view, see John Crispin (179-80). For more on circularity in the play, see Harriet S. Turner (*passim*).

[2] Bernarda's puritanical mentality and exaggerations resemble those of characters such as Amaranta and Fernanda in *Cien años de soledad* and Purísima del Carmen Vicario in *Crónica de una muerta anunciada*.

[3] See Katalin Kulin for various interesting possibilities regarding the symbolic significance of the mice and the relation of the mice to the lampoons (41).

[4] This situation also resembles that of Angela Vicario at the end of *Crónica de una muerte anunciada* when Angela finally frees herself from the influence of her mother and considers her only master to be Bayardo San Román. The similarity of the two men's names may not be a coincidence.

[5] Unlike Vargas Llosa, Michael Palencia-Roth interprets the lampoons as a "transición" from individual reality to collective reality, "porque se convierten en imagen de la colectividad" (45). In my judgment, both critics, are right; their views are compatible: "Lo cortés no quita lo valiente."

[6] Attuned to the mythological implications of the novel, Graciela Maturo convincingly argues that Pepe Amador, like Christ, is a scapegoat and that the mayor's attempt to make his body disappear is reminiscent of Christ's empty tomb (97).

[7] Numerous critics have commented on the play's imagery and symbolism; for an excellent overview of the play's symbolic language, see Ricardo Doménech (187-209).

[8] Pointing out that the mayor felt that he had dirty hands, Graciela Maturo affirms that the mayor's extraction of his tooth is linked to "un sentido de culpa que debe ser limpiada" (93). See also Luis Harss (408).

Chapter 2

Pragmatism and Other Pre-texts in
Cien años de soledad

I

Richard Rorty has suggested that the philosophy of pragmatism is the best foundation upon which to build a sound philosophy of language and, by extension, a comprehensive and workable theory of literature. Pragmatism rejects the "correspondence-to-reality" theory of truth, judging truth in terms of consequences or effects in relation to specific purposes and contexts. Propositional sentences, for example, create one kind of effect; non-propositional sentences create other kinds of effects. As Rorty affirms:

> Pragmatism cuts across this transcendental/empirical distinction by questioning the common presupposition that there is an invidious distinction to be drawn between kinds of truth. For the pragmatist, true sentences are not true because they correspond to reality, and so there is no need to worry about what sort of reality, if any, a given sentence corresponds to—no need to worry about what makes it true (*Consequences* xvi).

In Rorty's view, pragmatism not only transcended analytic philosophy, but also anticipated certain current philosophies of language:

> On my view, James and Dewey were not only waiting at the end of the dialectical road which analytic philosophy traveled, but are waiting at the end of the road which, for example, Foucault and Deleuze are currently traveling (*Consequences* xviii).

For the pragmatist, what is true depends on consequences, what works to achieve specific goals in a circumscribed context. The pragmatist rejects a priori truths, absolutes, metaphysics, rationalism, and the limitation of truth to what can be expressed through propositional language. Pragmatism stresses the importance of context, pluralism, concreteness, facts, the fluidity of experience, purpose, and the particular perspectives from which events are observed. The emphasis is on examples rather than principles or theories, though, as James writes, theories do possess instrumental value:

> *Theories thus become instruments, not answers to enigmas in which we rest.* We don't lie back upon them, we move forward, and, on occasion, make nature over again by their aid. Pragmatism unstiffens all our theories, limbers them up and sets each one at work (46-47).

The resolution of arguments upon which no practical difference in consequences hinge is rejected as sterile. James puts it this way:

> Pragmatism, on the other hand asks its usual question. "Grant an idea or belief to be true," it says, "what concrete difference will it make in any one's actual life? How will the truth be realized? What experiences will be different from those which would obtain if the belief were false? What, in short, is the truth's cash-value in experiential terms?"
>
> The moment pragmatism asks this question, it sees the answer: True ideas are those that we can assimilate, validate, corroborate and verify. False ideas are those that we can not" (133).

By focusing on effects, pragmatism minimizes the problem of discriminating between objective and subjective factors in the search for truth. Writing in *Contingency, Irony, and Solidarity*, of James's remarks on "'a certain blindness in human beings' to others inward perspectives," Rorty sees Freud as having refined our understanding of our blindness:

> I take Freud to have spelled out James's point in more detail helping us overcome particularly intractable cases of blindness by letting us see the 'peculiar ideality' of events which exemplify, for example, sexual perversion, extreme cruelty, ludicrous obsession,

and manic delusion. He lets us see each of these as the
private poem of the pervert, the sadist, or the lunatic:
each as richly textured and 'redolent of moral memories' as our own life. He lets us see what moral philosophy describes as extreme, inhuman, and unnatural as
continuous with our own activity. But, and this is the
crucial point, he does not do so in the traditional philo-
sophical reductionist way (38-39).

Literature, then, and especially the novel, exemplify
pragmatism *par excellence*. The multiple perspectives of the
novel, its Protean structure, the great variety of linguistic techniques it uses to achieve its effects, its great variety of discourses,
the collaboration required between the reader and the text, and
the novel's tendency to blur categories of all kinds combine to
make pragmatism an illuminating method for understanding
the nature and functions of the novel. There is nothing new in
this, of course. Writing of Dickens several decades ago, E. M.
Forster said that a novel can contain any number of flaws, but it
cannot be lacking in vitality, it must be "very clever at transmit-
ting force" (72). Pragmatism can help us understand how a
novel achieves it effects, how it comes off.

Because it rejects the "correspondence-to-reality" theory of
truth and the hegemony of propositional language, pragmatism
can shed light on the effects produced by "magical realism,"
which encompasses a wide variety of writing styles and blurs the
traditional distinctions between mimetic and fantastic elements
to create new effects through "defamiliarization." To the extent
that "magical realism" and *lo real maravilloso* "presuppose," to
use Jonathan Culler's word (114-18), pragmatism, this philosophy or method of determining what is true, constitutes a pre-text
for this style of writing.

Although other techniques are also involved, the "magical" inventions and "discoveries" of *Cien años de soledad* often
depend for their effects on the pragmatic test of truth. The
dramatization of these events nearly always entails exaggeration
and deception of some sort, but at the same time, from a given
perspective they are functionally true. The magnets with which
Melquíades astonishes the townspeople are a case in point:

Fue de casa en casa arrastrando dos lingotes metálicos,
y todo el mundo se espantó al ver que los calderos, las
pailas, las tenazas y los anafes se caían de su sitio y las
maderas crujían por la desesperación de los clavos y los

> tornillos tratando de desenclavarse y aun objetos perdi-
> dos desde hacía mucho tiempo aparecían por donde más
> se les había buscado, y se arrastraban en desbordada
> turbulenta detrás de los fierros mágicos de Melquíades.
> "Las cosas tienen vida propia—pregonaba el gitano con
> áspero acento—, todo es cuestión de despertarles el
> ánimo" (9).

The reader, of course, cannot accept the gypsy's claims as true because his language is at odds with that of regnant modern cos-
mologies. Melquíades's language does have the power to persuade Macondinos, however, because it is in harmony with their
pre-scientific presuppositions. From their perspective, it seems
reasonable to believe that things have a life of their own. Ultimately, however, when José Arcadio Buendía learns that the
magnets are useless for mining gold, he must modify his beliefs
about them. In so far as they fail to exemplify James's assertion
that "our beliefs are rules for action" (43), the magnets fail the
pragmatic test for truth.[1]

The same thing occurs with the huge magnifying glass
which, though it can start fires, proves useless as a weapon of
war. Again, José Arcadio Buendía thinks logically, but what
seems to follow logically proves not to be true in terms of consequences (10).

The incident involving the telescope exemplifies pragmatic truth from a different angle. Melquíades presents the telescope as one of the latest discoveries of the Amsterdam Jews:

> Sentaron una gitana en un extremo de la aldea e insta-
> laron el catalejo a la entrada de la carpa. Mediante el
> pago de cinco reales, la gente se asomaba al catalejo y
> veía a la gitana al alcance de su mano. "La ciencia ha
> eliminado las distancias," pregonaba Melquíades.
> "Dentro de poco, el hombre podrá ver lo que ocurre en
> cualquier lugar de la tierra sin moverse de su casa" (10).

At first glance, the gypsy's assertion that science has eliminated distance seems hyperbolic and witty, but absurd. On second thought, however, from one perspective it meets the pragmatic test of truth: considered from the standpoint of one of the
five senses, of which the telescope is an extension, it is true in
terms of its effect. Visually, the gypsy woman is near the ob-
server. Melquíades claim that science has eliminated distance is
false with respect to the other senses, but true in this one dimen-

sion. Melquíades' deception is based on the justifiable expectation that the Macondinos will accept the part for the whole, that they will think synecdochically.

His prediction that human beings will soon be able to observe events anywhere on earth from a single vantage point, meant to astonish his audience and, initially, the reader, exemplifies *lo real maravilloso*. Since the reader's initial reaction is likely to contain a strong element of incredulity, given his habituation to the gypsy's exaggerations, when he pauses to reflect, it dawns on him that in terms of visual and auditory effects satellite television has made Melquíades' absurd prediction true in not one but two sensory dimensions. Hence, the combination of exaggeration, deception, wit, and pragmatic truth produces in the reader a renewed sense of the miraculousness of all reality— *lo real maravilloso*.

Truths that cannot be confirmed pragmatically wither and die on the vine. The citizens of Macondo simply do not have the pre-text, the presuppositions and beliefs to accept as true José Arcadio Buendía's excited announcement: "La tierra es redonda como una naranja" (12). Ursula loses all patience with him:

> "Si has de volverte loco, vuélvete tú solo," gritó. "Pero no trates de inculcar a los niños tus ideas de gitano." José Arcadio Buendía, impasible, no se dejó amedrentar por la desesperación de su mujer, que en un rapto de cólera le destrozó el astrolabio contra el suelo (12).

In addition to revealing the wasteful repetitiveness of rediscovering what is already known in the civilized world, typical of isolated cultures, this incident also shows that, if they are to have an impact, such advances in knowledge must be prepared for and supported by a cultural tradition. Ursula assumes the point of view of common sense, which, as James said, is simply an embodiment of ready-made beliefs in language:

> *Our fundamental ways of thinking about things are discoveries of exceedingly remote ancestors, which have been able to preserve themselves throughout the experience of all subsequent time.* They form one great stage of equilibrium in the human mind's development, the stage of *common sense*. Other stages have grafted themselves upon this stage, but have never succeeded in displacing it (114).

In the same vein, James adds:

> There are thus at least three well-characterized lev-
> els, stages or types of thought about the world we live
> in, and the notions of one stage have one kind of merit,
> those of another stage another kind. It is impossible,
> however, to say that any stage yet in sight is abso-
> lutely more *true* than any other. Common sense is the
> more consolidated stage, because it got its innings first,
> and made all language its ally. Whether it or science
> be the more *august* stage may be left to private judg-
> ment. But neither consolidation nor augustness are deci-
> sive marks of truth (124).

Not only does James's understanding of the relations between
language, common sense, and truth expressed here seem compatible with García Márquez's operative views in *Cien años* but
they also seem to have anticipated the philosophy of language
upon which intertextuality is based. For this reason, Rorty, in
the passage cited above, asserted that "James and Dewey . . . are
waiting at the end of the road which, for example, Foucault and
Deleuze are currently traveling" (xviii).[2]

Melquíades's rejuvenation is another case of deception
based on the Macondinos synecdochical thinking. Since they
have never seen false teeth, it is natural for them to focus on
what is new and different in the gypsy's appearance. From their
perspective, he has regained his youth. To the extent that youth-
fulness is a matter of physical appearance, in the townspeople's
eyes Melquíades can control his age:

> De modo que todo el mundo se fue a la carpa, y mediante
> el pago de un centavo vieron un Melquíades juvenil, re-
> puesto, desarrugado con una dentadura nueva y radi-
> ante. Quienes recordaron sus encías destruidas por el
> escorbuto, sus mejillas fláccidas y sus labios marchitos
> se estremecieron de pavor ante aquella prueba termi-
> nante de los poderes naturales del gitano. El pavor se
> convirtió en pánico cuando Melquíades se sacó los di-
> entes, intactos, engastodos en las encías, y se los mostró
> al público por un instante—un instante fugaz un que
> volvió a ser el mismo hombre decrépito de los años ante-
> riores—y se los puso otra vez y sonrió de nuevo con un
> dominio pleno de su juventud restaurada (14).

The role perspective and context play in determining
what is perceived as true is further illustrated in the ice episode.

What constitutes common sense in an isolated and relatively primitive culture such as that of Macondo is different from the common sense of an advanced culture. Common sense is a pretext which varies from culture to culture. Never having experienced anything like ice, it is humorous but understandable that José Arcadio Buendía perceives its sparkling transparency as "el diamante más grande del mundo" (23) and that Aureliano experiences the pain of its coldness upon his hand as boiling hot (22). Their interpretations of the ice in terms of their beliefs by no means exhaust their reactions, however. Ultimately, the ice elicits in José Arcadio Buendía a sense of wonder and religious awe:

> Embriagado por la evidencia del prodigio, en aquel momento se olvidó de la frustración de sus empresas delirantes y del cuerpo de Melquíades abandonado al apetito de los calamares. Pagó otros cinco reales, y con la mano puesta en el témpano, como expresando un testimonio sobre el texto sagrado, exclamó:
> "Este es el gran invento de nuestro tiempo" (23).

In this context "el texto sagrado" is what causes wonder and reverence. The reader reacts to this episode with a sense of irony, humor, and, seeing the ice through the eyes of the two characters, with something of a sense of wonder. Ordinary ice is "defamiliarized," made strange, at least momentarily.

Through the use of the devices of "magical realism" throughout *Cien años* García Márquez attempts to place his readers in the same position vis-à-vis "ordinary reality" in which José Arcadio Buendía finds himself facing the ice, i.e., with a sense that what we think of as ordinary reality is a sacred text, an endless source of invention and mystery, characterized by Alejo Carpentier as *lo real maravilloso*. The reader's pragmatic truth, then, is different from that of the novel's characters in that it contains elements of irony and humor, but to a great extent it also coincides with theirs in giving rise vicariously to a strong element of wonder.

Two spectacles sponsored by the second group of gypsies are primarily based on the moral beliefs of the townspeople, but also on the psychology of resentment and simple curiosity about anything that is extraordinary. The first has to do with filial disobedience; it is "el triste espectáculo del hombre que se convirtió en víbora por desobedecer a sus padres" (35).[3] The second is "la prueba terrible de la mujer que tendrá que ser decaptiada todas las noches a esta hora durante ciento cincuenta años, como castigo por haber visto lo que no debía (35). Typically, García Márquez employs hyperbole and humor in satirizing traditional moralism. It is interesting to compare a more conventional treatment of this *motif* by García Lorca in *La casa de Bernarda Alba* when Bernarda exclaims to a neighbor whose daughter has rebelled against her parents: "Una hija que desobedece deja de ser hija para convertirse en una enemiga" (93). What in the Lorca play is an enemy becomes in García Márquez's novel, in a *reductio ad absurdum*, a monstrous freak. To what in Lorca's play is straightforward heartlessness, the Colombian writer adds a good dosage of humor. The implications of the episode involving the flying carpet are similar to those of the introduction in Macondo of the telescope:

> Una tarde se entusiasmaron los muchachos con la estera voladora que pasó veloz al nivel de la ventana del laboratorio llevando al gitano conductor y a vario niños de la aldea que hacían alegres saludos con la mano, y José Arcadio Buendía ni siquiera la miró. "Déjenlos que sueñen" dijo. "Nosotros volaremos mejor que ellos con recursos más científicos que ese miserable sobrecamas" (35).

José Arcadio Buendía's prediction "defamiliarizes" the flying machines that in fact science and technology have made possible, leading the reader to perceive that machines he takes for granted are indeed far superior in capabilities and comfort to the magical flying carpet.

One of pragmatism's presuppositions which Rorty stresses is the contingency of all starting points in the quest for truth. In Rorty's view a sense of community is developed through our conversation with each other, and the communities are "*ours* rather than *nature*'s, *shaped* rather than *found*, are among many which men have made" (*Consequences* 166). For Rorty, a fundamental doctrine of pragmatism is "that there are no constraints or inquiries save conversational ones—no wholesale constraints derived from the nature of the objects, or of the mind, or of language, but only those retail constraints provided by the remarks of our fellow-enquirers" (*Consequences* 166). Later, he adds: "The pragmatists tell us that the conversation which it is our moral duty to continue is merely our project . . ." (*Consequences* 173).

Implicit in José Arcadio Segundo's inculcation of Aureliano with his version of the banana company's activities is
keeping the conversation going, ensuring that the official version of the strike and massacre is not the only interpretation:

> Enseñó al pequeño Aureliano a leer y a escribir, lo inició
> en el estudio de los pergaminos, y le inculcó una inter-
> pretación tan personal de lo que significó para Macondo
> la compañía bananera, que muchos años después cuando
> Aureliano se incorpora al mundo, había de pensarse que
> contaba una versión alucinada, porque era radicalmente
> contraria a la falsa que los historiadores habían admi-
> tido, y consagrado en los textos escolares (296).

It is not flattering, of course, that Macondinos have accepted the
official version of the banana-strike massacre. The insinuation
remains that they, like the Germans who professed to know
nothing of the atrocities committed in concentration camps,
have stopped the conversation, whether out of fear, indifference,
or laziness. A significant result is the decadence of their spirit of
community or feeling of solidarity—in a word, their solitude.
On another level, of course, the novelist keeps the conversation
going.

To sum up, pragmatism figures as a pre-text in various
ways in *Cien años*. In instances such as the introduction of the
telescope, it serves to provide a basis in "reality" for what at first
glance appears primarily to be an attempt at deception. In other
cases, the narrator assumes the point of view, the cosmogony of
the characters so that fantastic spectacles, such as that of the man
transformed into a viper for disobeying his parents, within the
framework of the townspeople's beliefs constitutes a materializa-
tion of the consequences of filial disobedience. Notwithstanding
the irony that arises from the disparity between the characters'
points of view and that of the reader, the reader is led to an expanded perception of the nature of reality. For a host of reasons,
the reader is momentarily seduced by appearances, which involve an intricate blend of common-sense reality and fantasy.
The reader's perceptions and feelings are momentarily co-opted.
Expectations grow as to what is possible in the world; something
of the miraculousness of reality (*lo real maravilloso*) is recap-
tured. Moreover, the reader is led to understand, through assuming the characters' points of view, what they consider to be
pragmatically true. Consequently, to the extent that the reader's

feelings, imagination, and intellect are co-opted their truths become his truths.

II

Curiously, little has been said about the imprint of Lorca on García Márquez's work. Perhaps this is owing in part to the fact that the Colombian writer has seldom, if ever, mentioned the Spanish playwright as an influence or even as one of his favorite writers. Nevertheless, Lorca's *La casa de Bernarda Alba* is clearly a significant pre-text for *Cien años*, as well as for *La mala hora*. The psychological resemblances between certain characters created by the two writers coupled with strikingly similar incidents and situations constitute strong evidence that García Márquez was thoroughly familiar with the Lorca play and that he borrowed liberally from it, without this suggesting a lack of originality on his part. On the contrary, it is interesting to observe how he assimilates and adapts to his own purposes situations and incidents borrowed from the Spanish poet and playwright.

Characters in *Cien años*, such as Amaranta, Fernanda, and, at times, even Ursula, reveal a psychology closely resembling that of Bernarda Alba. Although it might be objected that since these characters are simply shaped in a common mold of ultraconservative Catholic moralism, the similarities reflect mere cultural affinities rather than conscious influence. Such an argument would be compelling, if it were not for the close similarities in both language and situations.

Notwithstanding the numerous positive qualities Ursula Iguarán possesses as matriarch of the Buendía clan, she fails in some respects to escape the mold of the traditional, puritanical Hispanic woman. Although ostensibly her homemade chastity belt is worn out of fear of giving birth to a child with a pig's tail, it also epitomizes ultraconservative Hispanic Catholics' traditional overvaluation of virginity. In this respect, Ursula is Bernarda Alba's literary soul sister. She also resembles Bernarda in her exaggerated observance of mourning. When Remedios Moscote dies after childbirth, Ursula arranges a period of mourning that Bernarda herself could have approved:

> Ursula dispuso un duelo de puertas y ventanas ce-
> rradas, sin entrada ni salida para nadie como no fuera
> para asuntos indispensables; prohibió hablar en voz
> alta durante un año y puso el daguerrotipo de Remedios
> en el lugar en que se veló el cadávar, con una cinta negra
> terciada y una lámpara de aceite encendida para siem-
> pre (82).

As in Lorca's play, this long and rigorous period of mourning produces nothing but frustration. Specifically, it means an indefinite postponement of Rebeca and Pietro Crespi's wedding. With the delay comes a change of circumstances that frustrates the wedding plans altogether and results in Pietro Crespi's suicide.

The mourning Bernarda imposes on her household after the death of her second husband is even more rigorous than that dictated by Ursula:

> En ocho años que dure el luto no ha de entrar en esta
> casa el viento de la calle. Hacemos cuenta que hemos
> tapiado con ladrillos puertas y ventanas. Así pasó en
> casa de mi padre y en casa de mi abuelo (25).

It should be noted, however, that the cult of death exemplified in Bernarda's attitude and acts is never balanced by life-affirming acts, Ursula's unthinking traditionalism is not pathological, and is more than compensated for by life-affirming acts.

Ursula displays the same fear of gossip (of *el qué dirán*) that afflicts Bernarda Alba when she would not permit her mother to go to the well in the patio for fear of her neighbors' gossip. When Colonel Aureliano Buendía leaves Macondo to fight the conservative government forces against Ursula's will, her reaction is extreme:

> Ursula pasó la tranca en la puerta decidida a no
> quitarla en el resto de la vida. "Nos pudriremos aquí
> dentro," pensó. "Nos volveremos ceniza en esta casa sin
> hombres, pero no le daremos a este pueblo miserable el
> gusto de vernos llorar" (154).

These words reveal the same atmosphere and the same psychology of rancor that exist in Bernarda's house and town.

Amaranta's repressed sexuality, which is expressed through frequent sexual play, just short of intercourse, with her nephews parallels the repressed sexuality of Bernarda. Bernarda declares that women attending mass should look at no man unless he is a priest. To do otherwise "es buscar el calor de la pana" (21). Poncia mutters to herself: "¡Sarmentosa por calentura de varón!" (21) Like Bernarda, Amaranta exalts virginity as the highest value, despite its destructive role in her life and in the lives of those around her. Before her death she insists that Ursula give public testimony of her virginity. Bernarda's overvaluation of virginity is just as destructive. After Adela is driven to suicide by her mother's actions, the latter shrieks three times that Adela "ha muerto virgen" (123). Bernarda and Amaranta have in common a hard pride that makes them inflexible where men are concerned. When Poncia points out to Bernarda that at thirty-nine Angustias has never had a suitor, her mistress angrily retorts: "¡No ha tenido novio [y] ninguno les hace falta! Pueden pasarse muy bien" (31). To Ursula's advice that she marry Colonel Gerineldo Márquez, Amaranta replies in the same vein as Bernarda: "No necesito andar cazando hombres . . ." (122).

In Fernanda's case, the influence of *Bernarda Alba* is evidenced in her psychological resemblance to Bernarda rather than the similarity of incidents; both women are extremely puritanical in sexual matters. Nevertheless, one cannot help but note that, like Bernarda with her daughters, Fernanda buries her daughter Meme in life, sending her to a distant convent. This occurs after Fernanda orders a guard to shoot Meme's suitor, Mauricio Babilonia, leaving him paralyzed for life, an event reminiscent of Bernarda's attempt to shoot Adela's lover, Pepe el Romano, as he flees in the night.

The thematic opposition sterility-fertility is dramatized in *Bernarda Alba* through the contrasting images of the daughters' entombment in Bernarda's house and the reapers' freedom and cheerfulness on their way to and from work (67-70). The opposition is further dramatized through Prudencia's observation that Bernarda has been able to increase her livestock (94) and through the demented María Josefa's ranting about "crías y crías y crías," symbolizing the deepest longings of Bernarda's daughters (111-14).

Characters such as Amaranta, Fernanda, and, occasionally, Ursula are juxtaposed with characters such as Pilar Ternera and Petra Cotes who, despite being "bad women," symbolize the plenitude of life and fertility. In this connection, a specific incident involving Petra Cotes and Aureliano Segundo is manifestly based on a similar incident in *Bernarda Alba*. During her visit with Bernarda, Prudencia is startled by the sound of a loud blow to the wall. Bernarda explains that the sound was made by "el caballo garañón, que está encerrado y da coces contra el muro" (94). The horse senses the presence of the young mares that Bernarda will mate with the stud the next morning, continuing thus to increase her livestock.

Typically, García Márquez's version involves a gross exaggeration. Petra Cotes raffles rabbits, which reproduce at an astonishing rate:

> Al principio, Aureliano Segundo no advirtió las alarmantes proporciones de la proliferación. Pero una noche cuando ya nadie en el pueblo quería oír hablar de las rifas de conejos, *sintió un estruendo en la pared del patio*. "No te asustes," dijo Petra Cotes. "Son los conejos." No pudieron dormir más, atormentados por el tráfago de los animales. Al amanecer, Aureliano Segundo abrió la puerta y vio el patio empedrado de conejos, azules en el resplandor del alba (167; emphasis added).

As noted above in the chapter on *La mala hora*, this is the second time García Márquez adapts the incident involving the stud horse to his purposes. Both adaptations are made within the framework of the sterility-fertility opposition.

In another adaptation of an incident in *Bernarda Alba*, García Márquez makes literal what is merely figurative in the play. In her insanity, María Josefa functions as a kind of Greek chorus, voicing truths that Bernarda would not allow her daughters to express. Mindful of the deficit psychology of the daughters, who overvalue Pepe el Romano because of their sexual and social frustrations, María Josefa utters these words: "Pepe el Romano es un gigante. Todas lo queréis. Pero él os va a devorar porque vosotras sois granos de trigo. No granos de trigo. ¡Ranas sin lengua!" (114).

In *Cien años*, José Arcadio, the man whose sexual attractiveness to women is so great that he raffles himself off to them, is literally a giant:

> Llegaba un hombre descomunal. Sus espaldas cuadradas apenas si cabían por las puertas. Tenía una medallita de la Virgen de los Remedios colgada en el cuello de bisonte, los brazos y el pecho completamente

bordados de tatuajes crípticos, y en la muñeca derecha
la apretada esclava de cobre de los *niños-en-cruz*. Tenía
el cuero curtido por la sal de la intemperie, el pelo corto
y parado como las crines de un mulo, las mandíbulas
férreas y la mirada triste. Tenía un cinturón dos veces
más grueso que la cincha de un caballo, botas con po-
lainas y espuelas y con los tacones herrados, y su presen-
cia daba la impresión trepidatoria de un sacudimiento
sísmico (83).

Frustrated by the delays of her wedding with Pietro Crespi, Rebeca succumbs immediately to José Arcadio's charms, thinking
that "Pietro Crespi era un currutaco de alfeñique junto a aquel
protomacho cuya respiración volcánica se percebía en toda la
casa (85). Again, in addition to literalizing Lorca's figurative description, García Márquez employs hyperbole.

III

The influence of William Faulkner on Latin American
novelists is extraordinary. Much has been written about the reasons for this influence, but perhaps the most succinct statement
has been made by Vargos Llosa in *A Writer's Reality*:

There are, of course, many reasons for a Latin American
writer to be influenced by Faulkner. First is the literary importance of Faulkner's work; he is probably the
most important novelist of our time, the most original,
the most rich. He created a world as rich as the richest
narrative worlds of the nineteenth century. But there
are more specific reasons for which Faulkner has such
appeal in Latin America. The world out of which he
created his own world is quite similar to a Latin American world. In the deep South, as in Latin America, two
different cultures coexist, two different historical traditions, two different races—all forming a difficult co-
existence full of prejudice and violence. There also exists the extraordinary importance of the past, which is
always present in contemporary life. In Latin America,
we have the same thing. The world of Faulkner is
preindustrial, or, at least, resisting industrialization,
modernization, urbanization—exactly like many Latin
American societies. Out of this, Faulkner created a personal world, with a richness of technique and form. It is

> understandable that to a Latin American who works
> with such similar sources, the techniques and formal
> inventions of Faulkner hold strong appeal (75-76).

Faulkner's influence on García Márquez has been well documented by critics such as Harvey D. Oberhelman, Susan Snell, Florence Delay, Jacqueline de Labrialle, Donald McGrady, and Gene H. Bell-Villada. The novelist himself has frequently indicated in interviews that Faulkner is one of his favorite writers (see, for example, *El olor de la guayaba*, 66). Although critics have often commented both on general and specific similarities between the two writers, they have missed a probable model for Remedios, la bella, in *The Hamlet*, the first novel of Faulkner's trilogy about the Snopes family. There are differences, of course. Unlike Remedios, la bella, Eula gets married—to Flem Snopes. Except for Remedios, la bella's *ascención*, Eula is presented in terms almost as exaggerated as those in which Remedios, la bella, is presented.

Both women have an immediate magnetic effect on the men with whom they come into contact; both emit a fragrance or possess an aura that has an immediate effect on men; both are indifferent to and unaware of the effect they produce on men, seeming not to understand the causes of the effect; and both are extremely lazy.

Remedios la bella's sexual attractiveness is presented largely in terms of the effects she has on men; Eula's sexual attractiveness is made explicit, albeit frequently within a mythical framework, as well as being described in terms of the effects she produces on men. Her extraordinary sexual development is emphasized in the first description we are given of her:

> Now, though not yet thirteen years old, she was al-
> ready bigger than most grown women and even her
> breasts were no longer the little, hard, fiercely-pointed
> cones of puberty or even maidenhood. On the contrary,
> her entire appearance suggested some symbology out of
> the old Dionysic times—honey in sunlight and bursting
> grapes, the writhen bleeding of the crushed fecundated
> vine beneath the hard rapacious trampling goat-hoof
> (95).

Her effect on the males at the school she attends is riveting and, again, described in mythological terms:

> By merely walking down the aisle between them she
> would transform the very wooden desks and benches
> themselves into a grove of Venus and fetch every male
> in the room, from the children just entering puberty to
> the grown men of nineteen and twenty, one of whom was
> already a husband and father, who could turn ten acres
> of land between sunup and sundown, springing into em-
> battled rivalry, importunate each for precedence in
> immolation (115).

The following passage reveals both Remedios la bella's disturb-
ing effects on men and her indifference to these effects:

> Hasta el último instante en que estuvo en la tierra ig-
> noró que su irreparable destino de hembra perturbadora
> era un desastre cotidiano. Cada vez que aparecía en el
> comedor, contrariando las órdenes de Ursula, ocasion-
> aba un pánico de exasperación entre los forasteros. Era
> demasiado evidente que estaba desnuda por completo
> bajo el burdo camisón, y nadie podía entender que su
> cráneo pelado y perfecto no era un desafío, y que no era
> una criminal provocación el descaro con que se chupaba
> los dedos después de comer con las manos (200).

The Hamlet contains a passage revealing a similar provocation,
involving the exposing of a thigh, and a similar indifference on
Eula's part. Since Eula is much too lazy to walk the half mile
from her home to school, her brother Jody rides with her each
day on horseback:

> He even decided one day that she should not ride
> astride anymore. This lasted one day, until he hap-
> pened to look aside and so behind him and saw the in-
> credible length of outrageously curved dangling leg and
> the bare section of thigh between dress and stocking-top
> looking as gigantically and profoundly naked as the
> dome of an observatory. And his rage was only intensi-
> fied by the knowledge that she had not deliberately
> exposed it. He knew that she simply did not care,
> doubtless did not even know it was exposed, and if she
> had known, would not have gone to the trouble to cover
> it (101).

Eula's innocence is further dramatized when Labove, the
schoolteacher, unsuccessfully attempts to force himself on her
when they are alone in the schoolroom (121-23). Despite the
fierce resistance she must put up to repel his advances, she tells

no one what has happened. Labove expects at worst to be shot by Jody, and at best to be fired, but nothing happens, because for Eula the incident was without importance; she failed to understand Labove's intentions. Labove eventually realizes why no one has sought revenge: "Yes, he thought quietly. Yes, I see. She never told him [Jody] at all. She didn't even forget to. She doesn't even know anything happened that was worth mentioning" (127).

Neither does Remedios, la bella, attach any significance to the men who attempt to force their attentions on her. When this occurs during an excursion to the new plantations, she tells no one:

> Remedios, la bella, no le contó a nadie que uno de los hombres, aprovechando el tumulto, le alcanzó a agredir el vientre con una mano que más bien parecía una garra de águila aferrándose al borde de un precipicio (203).

The incident which best exemplifies Remedios la bella's innocence, however, is the one in which a stranger climbs on the roof to watch her bathe. Undisturbed that the stranger should observe her bathing, her only concern is that he would seriously injure himself should he fall through the rotten tiles. Trying to maneuver into a position for a better look, the hapless man does fall, killing himself immediately (201-02). Eula's sexual attractiveness is made explicit, though her innocence is largely implicit in her acts or, better said, her attitude of indifference and her lack of action. Remedios la bella's innocence is made explicit, her sexuality remains implicit. Unlike Labove, who realizes that Eula is unaware of the effect she produces in men, Jody thinks his sister intentionally arouses men's interest in her by giving off an odor when they are around. When she accedes to his request to walk the short distance from the schoolhouse to the store to meet him, he exclaims that she gives off something to attract men:

> If you could arrange to have a man standing every hundred feet along the road, she would walk all the way home! She's just like a dog! Soon as she passes anything in long pants she begins to give off something. You can smell it ten feet away! (99).

Likewise, Remedios, la bella, emits an odor which, in her

case, lasts for hours. However, no one in her family is aware of it:

> Lo que ningún miembro de la familia supo nunca, fue que los forasteros no tardaron en darse cuenta de que Remedios, la bella, soltaba un hálito de perturbación, una ráfaga de tormento, que seguía pasado. Hombres expertos en trastornos de amor, probados en el mundo entero, afirmaban no haber padecido jamás una ansiedad semejante a la que producía el olor natural de Remedios, la bella. En el corredor de las begonias, en la sala de visitas, en cualquier lugar de la casa, podía señalarse el lugar exacto en que estuvo y el tiempo transcurrido desde que dejó de estar. Era un rastro definido, que nadie de la casa podía distinguir porque estaba incorporado desde hacía mucho tiempo a los olores cotidianos, pero que los forasteros identificaban de inmediato (200; see also 202-03).

Both Faulkner and García Márquez exaggerate the odor given off by these characters in order to dramatize the effect they produce on men. The odor, which on a smaller scale is certainly feasible, is an objective correlative of the attraction and anxiety that men feel around these two women.[4]

Both Eula and Remedios, la bella, are lazy and idle most of the time. In this respect Eula is more extreme than Remedios, la bella. As indicated above, Eula refuses to walk the half mile she lives from the schoolhouse. Initially, she is driven there in a surrey by a black man until Jody decides to take her with him on horseback. Eula is described as being "incorrigibly lazy" and complacent:

> She simply did not move at all on her own volition, save to and from the table and to and from bed. She was late in learning to walk. She had the first and only perambulator the countryside had seen, a clumsy expensive thing almost as large as a dog cart. She remained in it long after she had grown too large to straighten her legs out. When she reached the stage where it almost took the strength of a grown man to lift her out of it, she was graduated from it by force. Then she began to sit in chairs. It was not that she insisted upon being carried when she went anywhere. It was rather as though, even in infancy she already knew there was nowhere she wanted to go, nothing new or novel at the end of any progression, one place like another anywhere and everywhere (95).

When her father had the blacksmith make her a miniature per-
ambulator for her dolls, her parents finally realized "that her indifference to the toy was that she would have to move herself to
keep it in motion" (96).

Like Remedios, la bella, who seems simpleminded (204),
Eula is thought by her parents to be mentally backward until it
dawns on them that her indifference and inertia issue from
sheer laziness and a rare self-sufficiency (96). In addition to her
lack of interest in going anywhere, her self-sufficiency manifests
itself in her lack of friends:

> She had no playmates, no inseparable girl companion.
> She did not want them. She never formed one of those
> violent, sometimes short-lived intimacies in which two
> female children form embattled secret cabal against
> their masculine coevals and the mature world too. She
> did nothing. She might as well still have been a foetus
> (96).

Remedios la bella's laziness is evidenced in her decision to
shave her head in order not to have to take care of her hair and
her wearing of a rough, simple, tunic-like garment with nothing
under it. She dresses in this manner for comfort and the ease
with which it allows her to dress and undress (199). Ursula tries
in vain to interest her in the household tasks so that she will be
prepared for marriage:

> "Los hombres piden más de lo que tú crees," le decía
> enigmáticamente. "Hay mucho que cocinar, mucho que
> barrer, mucho que sufrir por pequeñeces, además de lo
> que crees." En el fondo se engañaba a sí misma tratando
> de adiestrarla para la felicidad doméstica, porque es-
> taba convencida de que una vez satisfecha la pasión, no
> había un hombre sobre la tierra capaz de soportar así
> fuera un día una negligencia que estaba más allá de
> toda comprensión (203-04).

Amaranta also fails in her attempt to train Remedios, la bella, in
practical skills and habits, concluding that her niece is simpleminded:

> Ya desde mucho antes, Amaranta había renunciado a
> toda tentativa de convertirla en una mujer útil. Desde
> las tardes olvidadas del costurero, cuando la sobrina
> apenas se interesaba por darle vuelta a la manivela de

> la máquina de coser, llegó a la conclusión simple de que
> era boba. "Vamos a tener que rifarte," le decía, per-
> pleja ante su impermeabilidad a la palabra de los
> hombres (204).

Ultimately, these two characters have quite different destinies. Eula becomes pregnant by an unidentified man, and her
father arranges a marriage between her and Flem Snopes, the
ambitious and unscrupulous newcomer who manages his store.
Remedios, la bella, of course, ascends into the heavens with the
aid of sheets hung out to dry. Such a divergence of ultimate destinies, however, cannot erase the striking similarities in the literary personalities of these two women. Although García
Márquez lives up to his reputation for hyperbole in his presentation of Remedios, la bella, it is evident that Faulkner also was
partial to a hyperbolic style, and it is likely that the Colombian
novelist picked up on this feature of his Mississippi mentor's
style.[5]

IV

García Márquez demonstrated an interest in the relation
between power and solitude at least as early as *La mala hora*
(1962, 1966) and as recently as *El general en su laberinto* (1989). It
is in *El otoño del patriarca* (1975), however, where he explores
the theme most thoroughly. In a conversation with Plinio
Apuleyo Mendoza, the novelist defines this novel as a "poema
sobre la soledad del poder" (*El olor* 122), further affirming that
"es un tema que ha estado latente en todas mis obras" (125).

In *El otoño*, the dictator is incapable of realizing all his
powers because he sees only one side of life and does not really
know who he is:

> . . . [Q]ue nunca había de ser dueño de todo su poder, que
> estaba condenado a no conocer la vida sino por el revés
> . . . un tirano de burlas que nunca supo dónde estaba el
> revés y dónde estaba el derecho de esta vida que
> amábamos con una pasión insaciable que usted no se
> atrevió ni siquiera a imaginar por miedo de saber lo que
> nosotros sabíamos de sobra que era ardua y efímera pero
> que no había otra, general, porque nosotros sabíamos
> quiénes éramos mientras él se quedó sin saberlo para
> siempre (270-71).

In *Cien años*, the character who most exemplifies the relation between power and solitude, continuing the exploration of the theme dealt with in *La mala hora* and anticipating the solitude of the tyrant in *El otoño*, is Colonel Aureliano Buendía. When the Colonel, who leads the liberal revolutionaries against the entrenched conservatives, himself commits a series of injustices, suggesting that there is no difference between liberals and conservatives, he realizes for the first time that he and his liberal associates are fighting for power alone (148).

After sentencing to death his companion-in-arms Colonel Gerineldo Márquez, and after Ursula threatens to kill him with her bare hands if he carries out the sentence, the Colonel feels the solitude of power: "[E]l coronel Aureliano Buendía rasguñó durante muchas horas, tratando de romperla, la dura cáscara de su soledad" (149). As in the case of *El otoño*'s general, the Colonel's solitude is augmented by an aura of myth surrounding him and all that he does: "Amaranta no lograba conciliar la imagen del hermano que pasó la adolescencia fabricando pescaditos de oro, con la del guerrero mítico que había interpuesto entre él y el resto de la humanidad una distancia de tres metros" (150). Physical isolation is a metaphor for the Colonel's psychological and social isolation. Moreover, he is also alienated from his past self. For this reason he burns the verses he had composed in a more sensitive stage of his life before his feelings were corrupted by his obsession with power (155). Observing Ursula's pitiful physical decadence, the Colonel realizes that his feelings are dead, that "esos estragos no suscitaban en él ni siquiera un sentimiento de piedad. Hizo entonces un último esfuerzo para buscar en su corazón el sitio donde se le habían podrido los afectos, y no pudo encontrarlo" (152).

A momentary stylistic shift in *Cien años* anticipates the style of *El otoño*. It consists of a long litany of complaints voiced by Fernanda. Slightly more than two pages in length, commas are the only punctuation until the period at the end of the diatribe (273-76).

A minor case of intertextuality involving certain features in both "El ahogado más hermoso del mundo" (1968), and "Un señor muy viejo con unas alas enormes" (1968), is the appearance two weeks after Ursula's death of a creature of indeterminable identity. The creature resembles the drowned man of "El ahogado" in being covered with "una costra de rémoras" and in being extraordinarily heavy even though he was no taller than an adolescent (292). Like the creature of "Un señor," he appears to have the characteristics of an angel in decadence; the narrator uses the phrase "ángel valetudinario" to describe him:

> Pesaba como un buey, a pesar de que su estatura no era mayor que la de un adolescente, y de sus heridas manaba una sangre verde y untuoso. Tenía el cuerpo cubierto de una pelambre áspera, plagada de garrapatas menudos, y el pellejo petrificado por una costra de rémoras, pero al contrario de la descripción del párroco, sus partes humanas eran más de ángel valetudinario que de hombre, porque las manos eran tersas y hábiles, los ojos grandes y crepusculares, y tenía en los momoplatos los muñones cicatrizados y callosos de unas alas potentes, que debieron ser desbastadas con hachas de labrador (292).

It is noteworthy that both incidents involve a confounded priest. The description of the angel in "un señor" is much more elaborate, but citation of a brief passage should suffice to demonstrate the similarities:

> Estaba vestido como un pordiosero. Le quedaban apenas unas hilachas descoloridas en el cráneo pelado y muy pocos dientes en la boca, y su lastimosa condición de bisabuelo ensopado lo había desprovisto de toda grandeza. Sus alas de gallinazo grande, sucias y medio desplumadas estaban encalladas para siempre en el lodazal (11-12).

This creature also is afflicted with parasites (15).

One of José Arcadio Buendía's projects is reminiscent of Borges "Funes el memorioso," a story in *Ficciones*. José Arcadio Buendía decides to build a memory machine which not only resembles some of Funes's projects, but also in a somewhat crude fashion "anticipates" the computer. Once again, the miraculousness of a reality we take for granted is dramatized through "defamiliarization" and irony.

> José Arcadio Buendía decidió entonces construir la máquina de la memoria que una vez había deseado para acordarse de los maravillosos inventos de los gitanos. El artefacto se fundaba en la posibilidad de repasar todas las mañanas, y desde el principio hasta el fin, la totalidad de los conocimientos adquiridos en la vida. Lo imaginaba como un diccionario giratorio que un indi-

> viduo situado en el eje pudiera operar mediante una
> manivela de modo que en pocas horas pasaron frente a
> los ojos las nociones más necesarias para vivir. Había
> logrado escribir cerca de catorce mil fichas . . . (48).

Compare the description of José Arcadio Buendía's project to passages about Funes's projects:

> Me dijo que hacia 1886 había discurrido un sistema
> original de numeración y que en muy pocas días había
> rebasado el veintiocho mil . . . (489).
> Resolvió reducir cada una de sus jornadas pretéritas
> a unos setenta mil recuerdos que definiría luego por
> cifras (489).[6]

Another minor case of intertextuality, in this instance an anticipation of an incident in *El amor en los tiempos del cólera* (1985), is found in the principal criterion Ursula uses to make a guest list for a party she organizes. With the exception of Pilar Ternera's family the list is composed exclusively of descendants of the founders of Macondo:

> Ursula hizo una lista severa de los invitados, en la cual
> los únicos escogidos fueron los descendientes de los fun-
> dadores, salvo la familia de Pilar Ternera . . . (59).

In *El amor* Juvenal Urbino and Fermina Daza invite guests to a luncheon who, at first glance, would seem incompatible because of their divergent political views. Yet on closer examination it turns out that what they all have in common is their aristocratic status in the community; they all belong to the oldest and most influential families in the city. The archbishop points out that they are making history in having political enemies sit at the same table. Juvenal Urbino resists the temptation to correct him:

> Aunque la habría gustado señalarle que nadie estaba en
> aquel almuerzo por lo que pensaba sino por los méritos
> de su alcurnia, y ésta habría estado siempre por encima
> de los azares de la política y los honores de la guerra.
> Visto así, en efecto no faltaba nadie (54).

Both these incidents imply a criticism of the class structure in Spanish America, revealing that such exclusiveness is yet another source of solitude, an impediment to solidarity.

Given the similarities in certain aspects of the description of the trains in *Cien años* and Galdós's *Doña Perfecta* (1876), it seems quite feasible that García Márquez was influenced by the Spanish novelist in his invention of the arrival of the first train in Macondo. In both novels the train is presented as an enormous panting beast that inspires fear in the hearts of those who hear its terrifying whistle.

In *Doña Perfecta* the train heralds the progress so feared and resisted by the reactionary inhabitants of Orbajosa and its environs. In *Cien años* the train also portends great changes, appearing superficially as progress, but which turn out to be primarily exploitive. Here is Galdós description of the train leaving Villahorrenda:

> Sus pasos, retumbando cada vez más lejanos, producían ecos profundos bajo tierra. Al entrar en el túnel de Kilómetro 172 lanzó el vapor por el silbato, y un aullido estrépitoso resonó en los aires. El túnel echando por su negra boca un hálito blanquecino clamoreaba como una trompeta, y al oir su enorme voz despertaban aldeas, ciudades, provincias. Aquí cantaba un gallo, más allá otro. Principiaba a amanecer (71).

In *Cien años* the description begins with an original and humorous image followed by images similar to those in *Doña Perfecta*:

> —Ahí viene—alcanzó a explicar—un asunto espantoso como una cocina arrastrando un pueblo.
> En ese momento la población fue estremecida por un silbato de resonancias pavorosas y un descomunal respiración acezante (192-93).

Dona Perfecta, as well as *Bernarda Alba* (as indicated above), could be the source of the episode in which Fernanda orders a guard to shoot Mauricio Babilonia, Meme's hapless suitor (248). It is Doña Perfecta, of course, who orders Caballuco to shoot her own nephew, Pepe Rey, after he stealthily entered her garden to meet her daughter Rosario. Moreover, both Rosario and Meme are destroyed by the respective fates of their suitors; Rosario becomes insane and is sent to an insane asylum; Meme enters a deep depression, refusing to talk, and she is figuratively buried alive in a convent in Krakow.

Notes

[1] In view of García Márquez's frequent claim that everything he writes is based on reality, it is interesting to note that Thomas A. Edison and a partner lost more than a million dollars in New Jersey in a scheme to separate iron from ore with a large electrified magnet.

[2] James's description of stages existing side by side and applicable to different spheres is remarkably similar to Thomas Kuhn's (*The Structure of Scientific Revolutions*) view of scientific paradigms which are not necessarily cast aside, but are applied to different areas or levels of the external world.

[3] This situation anticipates the predicament in "Un señor muy viejo con unas alas enormes" of the young woman who turned into a spider for disobeying her parents.

[4] Although García Márquez's almost systematic exaggeration of his borrowings serves many purposes, one obvious result is to disguise his sources and thereby reduce any "anxiety of influence" he might feel.

[5] Another stylistic feature for which both writers have demonstrated a fondness is the coordinate-conjunction construction, dealt with in the last chapter. For multiple examples in *The Hamlet*, see pp. 208-14.

[6] One cannot help but wonder if in his creation of Funes Borges was influenced by Charles Sanders Peirce's astonishing schemes in semiotics. According to Jonathan Culler, Peirce developed a "taxonomy yielding a possible 59,049 classes of sign," as well as a "swarm of neologisms" (23). Compare Funes's project of assigning each number an individual name.

Chapter 3

Echoes of the *Iliad* in
Crónica de una muerte anunciada

In his Nobel lecture in 1982 García Márquez spoke of Latin America's "outsized" and "unbridled reality," explaining that "our crucial problem has been a lack of conventional means to render our lives believable" (89). Over the years the Colombian writer has had recourse to a variety of techniques and styles successfully to render Latin America comprehensible and believable. One style, of course, is magical realism, of which he is now considered by most critics to be the most masterful practitioner principally, but not exclusively, because of the critical success of *Cien años de soledad*. Whatever style he employs, and although García Márquez's novels and stories are replete with intertexts, ranging from the obvious to the extremely subtle, mythological allusions and parallels, especially Greek mythology, constitute one of the most frequent types. The richness of Greek mythology, its reflection of the initial stages of a culture in which our contemporary western culture is rooted, its universality, and its dramatic presentation of an outsized and unbridled reality make it especially appealing and useful to García Márquez both in his efforts to render Latin America comprehensible and as a writer of universal resonance. Stories in which, as Edith Hamilton has said, "little distinction had as yet been made between the real and the unreal" (3), have a special attraction to García Márquez with his fondness for blurring such distinctions. Moreover, the Colombian writer, with his Caribbean sensibility, must feel a natural affinity with the world of Greek mythology so at variance with the austerity of the ultraconservative Catholicism dominant in the Colombia and Latin America in which he grew up.   Although she is mindful of the occasional pettiness and cruelty of the Greek deities, Edith Hamilton nevertheless stresses their humanly attractiveness:

> On earth, too, the deities were exceedingly and humanly attractive. In the form of lovely youths and maidens they peopled the woodland, the forest, the rivers, the sea, in harmony with fair earth and the birth waters.
> That is the miracle of Greek mythology—a humanized world, men freed from the paralyzing fear of an omnipotent Unknown, the terrifying incomprehensibilities which were worshiped elsewhere, and the fearsome spirits with which earth, air, and sea swarmed were barred from Greece (9-10).

In book-length studies Graciela Maturo and Michael Palencia-Roth have amply documented and studied many of the mythological elements in García Márquez's narrative. My focus here is primarily, but not exclusively, on the parallels with and adaptations of certain aspects of Homer's the *Iliad* present in García Márquez's *Crónica de una muerte anunciada* (1981). My procedure will be to go from specific to more general intertexts.

The fear of being devoured by dogs after defeat in battle is expressed throughout the *Iliad*, and appears even in the opening lines of the epic. Referring to the consequences of Achilles's anger, the narrator announces in the opening lines: "Many a hero did it yield a prey to dogs and vultures . . ." (7). Priam, king of Troy and father of Hector, lamenting his probable fate, expresses this same feeling of horror shortly before Achilles challenges Hector to engage in battle:

> In the end fierce hounds will tear me to pieces at my own gates after someone has beaten the life out of my body with sword and spear—hounds that I myself reared and fed at my own table to guard my gates, but who will yet lap my blood and then be all distraught at my doors (338).

Mortally wounded by Achilles, Hector pleads with his vanquisher to "let not the dogs devour me," promising that his mother and father will offer him a generous ransom if he will deliver his body to them unmutilated (344). But the vengeful Achilles, remembering the death and despoiling of his friend and comrade Patroclus, remains unmoved. He torments Hector telling him that "nothing shall save you from the dogs" and that "dogs and vultures shall eat you utterly up" (345; see also 287, 289, 290, 337, 338, 349).

In *Crónica* García Márquez imitates the fear of post-mortem mutilation by dogs so frequently expressed in the *Iliad* to intensify the feeling of horror associated with death. For both writers, such a feeling is both an integral part of their characters' psychology and an extremely effective rhetorical device for engaging their readers' interest. The first reference to dogs in *Crónica* also occurs early in the novel and serves to anticipate Santiago Nasar's death and mutilation. When Santiago enters the kitchen, the cook, Victoria Guzmán, surrounded by panting dogs is preparing three rabbits for lunch. Interviewing her many years later, the narrator describes her recollection of the scene:

> Pero no pudo eludir una ráfaga de espanto al recordar el horror de Santiago Nasar cuando ella arrancó de cuajo las entrañas de conejo y les tiró a los perros el tripajo humeante.
> —No seas bárbara—le dijo él—Imagínate que fuera un ser humano (18).

This is exactly what Victoria Guzmán begins to do, provoking Santiago with malice aforethought. Like Achilles, she is motivated by resentment and the desire for revenge. For many years she had been the mistress of Santiago's father until he finally tired of her. Also, she resents Santiago because of his lustful designs on her daughter Divina Flor. For these reasons she continues to feed the dogs the rabbit entrails just to spoil Santiago's breakfast:

> Sin embargo, tenía tantas rabias atrasadas la mañana del crimen, que siguió cebando a los perros con las vísceras de los otros conejos, sólo por amargarle el desayuno a Santiago Nasar (18).

That this episode anticipates and retrospectively intensifies the feeling of horror associated with Santiago's death is evident when the dying young man enters that same kitchen in which Victoria Guzmán had cleaned the rabbits and thrown their intestines to the dogs. As he enters, Santiago's own intestines are protruding from his abdomen and the smell drives the dogs wild with excitement:

> Además, los perros alborotados por el olor de la muerte
> aumentaban la zozobra. No habían dejado de aullar
> desde que yo entré en la casa, cuando Santiago Nasar
> agonizaba todavía en la cocina, y encontré a Divina
> Flor llorando a gritos y manteniéndoles a raya con una
> tranca.
> —Ayúdame—me gritó—, que lo que quieren es com-
> erse las tripas (116).

Although the dogs are locked up, the threat continues:

> Pero hacia el mediodía, nadie supo cómo, se escaparon
> de donde estaban e irrumpieron enloquecidos en la casa.
> Plácida Linero [Santiago's mother], por una vez perdió
> los estribos.
> —¡Estos perros de mierda!—gritó. ¡Que los maten!
> La orden se cumplió de inmediato, y la casa volvió a
> quedar en silencio (116-17).

Neither Hector, whose body the gods restore to its original appearance, nor Santiago fall prey to the dogs, though Santiago's
body is mutilated beyond recognition during the autopsy—of
which more below.

The presence of the *Iliad* in *Crónica* is revealed not only
in the detailed, hair-raising descriptions of Santiago's death and
the mutilation of his body but also in quite a specific way on at
least one occasion. What follows is one of the many instances in
which Homer provides graphic details of the death of a warrior,
the most gruesome detail of which is imitated by García Márquez
in *Crónica*. This passage describes the death of Polydorus, son of
Priam and brother of Hector, at the hands of Achilles. Polydorus
is the youngest and best-loved of Priam's sons:

> [Polydorus] in his folly and showing off the fleetness of
> his feet, was rushing about among the front ranks until
> he lost his life, for Achilles struck him in the middle of
> the back as he was darting past him—he struck him
> just at the golden fastenings of his belt and where the
> two pieces of the double breastplate overlapped. The
> point of the spear pierced him through and came out by
> the naval, whereon he fell groaning on to his knees and
> a cloud of darkness overshadowed him as he sank hold-
> ing his entrails in his hands.
> When Hector saw his brother Polydorus with his
> entrails in his hands and sinking down upon the ground,
> a mist came over his eyes, and he could no longer keep
> at a distance (318).

What for Polydorus is a "cloud of darkness" is for Santiago a hallucinatory state: "Se incorporó de medio lado, y se echó a andar en un estado de alucinación, sosteniendo con las manos las vísceras colgantes" (189). In both cases there are witnesses to the horrifying scene. Santiago is first seen by neighbors, whose breakfast he interrupts when he enters their house: "Empezaban a desayunar cuando vieron entrar a Santiago Nasar empapado de sangre llevando en las manos el racimo de sus entrañas" (189-90). Then the narrator's aunt Wenefrida Márquez observes his movements from the patio of her house across the river where she is scaling a fish: 'Hasta tuvo el cuidado de sacudir con la mano la tierra que le quedó en las tripas,' me dijo mi tía Wene" (191; see also 184).

The description of the murder itself is long, detailed, and gruesome (185-91), even more detailed than any single death described in the *Iliad*. In Homer the descriptions occur frequently and make up in quantity what they lack in length (for a few examples, see 68, 73-74, 81, 82, 83, 86, 154-55, 164, 206, 252, 255-56).

Achilles' pursuit of Hector outside the walls of Troy, as Randolph D. Pope has noted (190), offers interesting parallels with Santiago Nasar's desperate effort to reach the safety of his home. Both heroes' deaths are witnessed by a large gathering of people, and both heroes attempt to reach the safety of a door or gate. Hector seeks the aid of his compatriots within the city walls:

> . . . [T]here was no escape for Hector from the fleet son of Peleus. Whenever he made a set to get near the Dardanian gates and under the walls, that his people might help him by showering down weapons from above, Achilles would gain on him back towards the plain, keeping himself always on the city side (341).

Passing through the town square where nearly everyone in the town is assembled to witness the murder, Santiago tries to reach the door of his house that opens on the square. Seconds before he reaches it, his mother Plácida Linero, assured by Divina Flor that her son had already entered the house, locks the door. Santiago runs through the square toward the door at an angle that makes him invisible to his mother:

> Santiago necesitaba apenas unos segundos para entrar cuando se cerró la puerta. Alcanzó a golpear varias

veces con los puños, y en seguida se volvió para en-
frentarse a manos limpias con sus enemigos (185).

When Bayardo San Román asks Angela Vicario which
house she likes best, she replies that "la más bonita del pueblo
era la quinta del viudo de Xius" (56). The name Xius appears to
be a transformation of the name Zeus, king of the Greek gods. In
fact, Xius's house, reminiscent of Zeus's home high on Mt.
Olympus, is situated high on a windswept hill overlooking the
marshes and the Caribbean Sea:

> Estaba en una colina barrida por los vientos, y desde la
> terraza se veía el paraíso sin límites de las ciénagas cu-
> biertas de anémonas moradas, y en los días claros del
> verano se alcanzaba a ver el horizonte nítido del
> Caribe, y los trasatlánticos de turistas de Cartagena de
> Indias (56).

Bayardo San Román offers Xius such a large amount for
the house that the widower, who had been so happy there with
his wife Yolanda, tearfully assents to sell it. Symbolically,
Bayardo San Román's purchase of Xius's home represents the
replacement of the pagan Greco-Roman gods with the God of
Roman Catholicism. The happy memories Xius associates with
his home on the hill contrast sharply with the disastrous
wedding-night scene created by its new owner. The contrast
dramatizes the superiority of Greek religion (or mythology) in its
attitude of acceptance and glorification of the human body to
ultraconservative Catholicism with its emphasis on instinctual
renunciation.

It is hardly accidental that Pedro and Pablo Vicario are hog
butchers by trade. Their profession and the fact that they murder
Santiago Nasar with rusty, homemade knives used in butchering hogs is in keeping with García Márquez's degradation of
Homeric myths in order to launch a sly attack on austere
Catholic morality. The *Iliad* describes the conflicts among gods,
demigods, and heroes. Their armor and weapons are magnifi-
cent and are often, as in Achilles's case, fashioned by the gods
themselves (294). They fight fiercely and without mercy, but also
nobly, against worthy opponents equally well armed. Santiago is
presented as the noble scion of a distinguished family, as a Christ
figure, and, most probably, as an innocent victim (suggested in
part by his white linen suit) of a decadent moral code. Although

the twins' replacement of the knives taken from them by Lázaro Aponte reflects the exigencies of realism, because of the emphasis placed on the nature and original function of the knives, it also contributes to the degradation of the myth:

> Clotilde Armenta no había acabado de vender la leche cuando volvieron los hermanos Vicario con otros dos cuchillos envueltos en periódicos. Uno era de descuartizar, con una hoja oxidada y dura de doce pulgadas de largo por tres de ancho, que había sido fabricado por Pedro Vicario con el metal de una segueta. . . . El otro era más corto, pero ancho y curvo. El juez instructor lo dibujó en el sumario, tal vez porque no lo pudo describir, y se arriesgó apenas a indicar que parecía un alfanje en miniatura. Fue con estos cuchillos que se cometió el crimen, y ambos eran rudimentarios y muy usados (94).

Thus, our hero's life was ended by crude, ignoble weapons wielded by practitioners of a humble trade, a far cry from the bloody, but noble, duels described in the *Iliad*.

Just as Helen of Troy is the cause of the Trojan war, so is Angela Vicario the cause of the conflict and murder of Santiago Nasar in *Crónica*. Although Angela is not considered a beauty, she is said to be the prettiest of the four Vicario sisters, and a detail furnished by the narrator's mother associates her indirectly with Helen, who was the wife of Menelaus, king of Sparta: "Angela era la más bella de las cuatro, y mi madre decía que había nacido como las grandes reinas de la historia con el cordón umbilical enrollado en el cuello" (50). Yet another Greek myth, related to Helen, but only indirectly related to the *Iliad*, through Helen, is echoed in the role played by the twins Pedro and Pablo. Their avenging of Angela (symbolically Helen) parallels the story of the twins Castor and Pollux's rescue of their sister Helen, who had been kidnapped by Theseus. When the kidnapping occurred, the future heroine of Troy was still a child. Theseus planned to marry her when she was grown. Edith Hamilton describes the rescue:

> Helen's brothers were Castor and Pollux, more than a match for any mortal hero. Theseus succeeding in kidnapping the little girl, just how we are not told, but the two brothers marched against the town she had been taken to and got her back. Luckily for him they did not find Theseus there (219).

Pedro and Pablo Vicario are certainly not gods, but because of their given names, their surname, and the ideology (theology?) animating their act of revenge, their role as God's representatives on earth is relatively transparent. In presenting his representatives of God as lowly hog butchers and wielders of crude and rusty knives, García Márquez clearly parodies and demythologizes the Greek myth. At the same time, he shows how they contribute, as unconscious instruments of the town's collective values, to the degradation of Christianity, that is, to the degradation of its original message of love, forgiveness, and promise of abundant life. Homer's Greeks place a high value on the human body, glorifying it in life and striving forcefully to preserve its integrity after death. For this reason, opposing warriors taunt each other with threats of mutilation and of throwing each other's bodies to the dogs. Thus we read that Achilles attempted to mutilate Hector's body, albeit in the end the gods intervene to restore the Trojan hero's body to a presentable state:

> On this he treated the body of Hector with contumely: he pierced the sinews at the back of both his feet from heel to ankle and passed thongs of oxhide through the slits he had made; thus he made the body fast to his chariot, letting the head trail upon the ground. Then when he had put the goodly armor on the chariot and had himself mounted, he lashed his horses on and they flew forward nothing loth. The dust rose from Hector as he was being dragged along, his dark hair flew all abroad, and his head once so comely was laid low on earth, for Zeus had now delivered him into the hands of his foes to do him outrage in his own land (346).

Just as Santiago's death and the mutilation of his body left in their wake a grieving mother and a town "espantado de su propio crimen" (187), Hector's death and the mutilation of his body leave his mother and father distraught with grief and a city overwhelmed with weeping and wailing:

> Thus was the head of Hector being dishonored in the dust. His mother tore her hair, and flung her veil from her with a loud cry as she looked upon her son. His father made a piteous moan, and throughout the city the people fell to weeping and wailing (346).

In addition to the horrible mutilation of Santiago's body during the murder itself (185-91), his body, like those of his mythological forebears, suffers mutilation after death, during the autopsy. Performed by Father Carmen Amador, a priest with some medical training in Salamanca, the autopsy "fue un masacre . . . (118). The priest himself described the autopsy to the narrator: "'Fue como si hubiéramos vuelto a matarlo después de muerto'" (114). Grieving over Santiago's cruel fate, the narrator expresses the following thought: "Pensaba en la ferocidad del destino de Santiago Nasar, que le había cobrado 20 años de dicha no sólo con la muerte, sino además con el descuartizamiento del cuerpo, y con su dispersión y exterminio" (123).   On the symbolic level of meaning, Santiago's death, mutilation, and the extermination and dispersal of his body have as a necessary cause the Church's traditional doctrine of the mortification of the flesh (or instinctual renunciation).   Instinctual renunciation, especially the overvaluation of virginity, is a logical consequence of this doctrine, Santiago Nasar is murdered, then, because Pedro and Pablo Vicario, who are more or less unconscious instruments of the townspeople, believe he has violated his code of honor, whose content is largely the belief in the sanctity of virginity.   In the mutilation that occurs both as a part of and after the murder, García Márquez employs hyperbole and irony to stress the Church's hostility to the body.   The irony lies in Father Amador and the townspeople's expectations of finding the cause of death in Santiago's body.   The real cause of his death is to be found in the town's collective psyche, the townspeople's unthinking and often inconsistent assimilation of the Church's hatred of the body.

In Homer the body is glorified, and attempts to kill, maim, and mutilate the body after death stem from conscious hostility and the spirit of revenge brought on by war.   The love of the body is a conscious value in these acts of revenge. In *Crónica*, on the other hand, while the motive of revenge certainly exists, much evidence exists in the novel that the twins hoped they would be stopped from committing the crime, once they had demonstrated their intent to avenge their sister's honor. Unlike in the *Iliad*, in *Crónica* there is hidden in the townspeople's psychology a complex pathology deriving from the Church's teachings, but which is also alloyed with self-interest. Moreover, the ambivalence felt by many of the townspeople with respect to the validity of the code of honor and the role self-interest plays in the failure to stop the murder (think of Victoria Guzmán) re-

veals how some individuals consciously or unconsciously per-
petuate the code of honor because it is in their interest to do so.
The general pattern of events in *Crónica* reveals a criticism of
the Christian degradation of the body in contrast with its glorification in the *Iliad*. In this particular regard, for García Márquez,
traditional Catholicism hardly represents an advance in religion's service to humanity, but rather a degradation of an earlier
more healthy attitude toward the body.

Fate reveals a strong presence in both the *Iliad* and
Crónica. Although Homer's heroes strive mightily to work
their will in human affairs, their final destinies, as well as many
of the details of their lives, are ordained by the gods. They often
seem to be free, but the narrator reminds us intermittently that
although the gods often release the strings attached to these human puppets, they are watchful of their conduct and seize the
strings again at critical junctures to ensure their ultimate control
over human events. We know, for instance, that the Achaeans
will ultimately triumph over the Trojans and that Achilles will
defeat Hector, but we are not told when or how this will happen.
Similarly, in *Crónica* we know from the first page that Santiago
Nasar is to be killed. But we are not told how, and more impor-
tantly, in this work, why. The ostensible reason for his death of
having deflowered Angela Vicario is much less important than
the hidden causes discussed above. In *Crónica*, then, unlike in
the *Iliad*, fate is largely internal rather than external. Fate
consists of a combination of individual character, collective
character, and chance. Chance alone, however, could not have
operated to produce Santiago's death. The necessary, but not
sufficient, cause of his death was the twins' and the townspeople's adherence to the code of honor. This code of honor, as
indicated above, is based on the Church's teachings, but compli-
cated by self-interest. Chance and coincidence come into play
largely after the brothers have made the decision to kill Santiago.
García Márquez's understanding of fate, then, is modern and
sophisticated, taking into account the distinction between reasons (conscious) and causes (unconscious or hidden). For the
Colombian writer, fate is the result of a complex interplay of external and internal forces: individual and collective character,
conscious and unconscious psychology, beliefs and ideology, self-
interest, and chance. Moreover, causality operates on various
levels. So complex is the operation of causality in the novel that
the reader may become fatigued and tempted to chalk it all up to

another case of indeterminacy. The coherence of the novel's symbolic level of meaning, however, seriously undermines such an interpretation.

The language of a fate as ineluctable as that of the *Iliad* appears throughout *Crónica*. The novel's title itself suggests the role of fate in bringing about the murder. Santiago's namesake Luisa Santiago refers to him as "el muerto" (38). Describing Angela Vicario's naming of Santiago Nasar as the man who deflowered her, the narrator says that she left him "clavado en la pared con su dardo certero, como a una mariposa sin albedrío cuya sentencia estaba escrita desde siempre" (76). On another occasion, thinking of the many people who knew the twins intended to kill Santiago, the narrator exclaims: "Nunca hubo una muerte más anunciada" (81). For years afterwards the townspeople talk about and reenact the crime, trying to determine the role fate had assigned to each of them in the matter:

> . . . [Y] era evidente que no lo hacíamos por un anhelo de esclarecer misterios, sino porque ninguno de nosotros podía seguir viviendo sin saber con exactitud cuál era el sitio y la misión que le había asignado la fatalidad (152).

When the presiding judge learned that even though virtually everyone was in the town square no one saw Santiago enter Flora Miguel's house at 6:45, he pens in the margin of his summary: "La fatalidad nos hace invisibles" (178).

In the *Iliad* the reader is led directly to perceive the working of fate in the announced intentions of the gods. The characters become aware of the role of fate in their lives retrospectively. When Achilles is pursuing Hector outside the Trojan walls, the goddess Athene persuades the Trojan hero to cease running and turn to challenge his opponent. Having hurled his only spear in vain at Achilles, Hector realizes that the gods have delivered him into the hands of his enemy:

> Alas the gods have lured me on to my destruction. I deemed that the hero Deïphobus was by my side, but he is within the wall, and Athene has inveigled me; death is now exceedingly near at hand and there is no way out of it—for so Zeus and his son Apollo, the far-darter have willed it, though heretofore they have been ever ready to protect me. My doom has come upon me; let me not then die ingloriously and without a

> struggle, but let me first do some great thing that shall
> be told among men hereafter (343-44).

Santiago Nasar enjoys no such moment of recognition. Although he is offered as a sacrifice on the altar of the God of ultra-conservative Catholicism, just as valuable animals are sacrificed by Homer's Greeks in attempts to sway or appease their gods, he appears to remain unaware of the reason for his death until the end. Santiago's fate is not in the hands of the gods, but rather is brought about by those who symbolically are God's earthly vicars (hence the surname Vicario).

In *Crónica* García Márquez has appropriated details as well as significant elements of the *Iliad*, adapting them to his own purposes. The overall effect is to universalize the significance of what happens in *Crónica*, giving the events an atemporal status as well as historicizing them through the contemporary setting. Moreover, the presence of ancient mythical models provides running opportunities for comparison and contrast with contemporary modes of being.

Chapter 4

Carnivalized Discourse in *Cien años de soledad* and *Crónica de una muerte anunciada*

An essential manifestation of García Márquez's "dialogic imagination" in *Cien años de soledad* (1967) and *Crónica de una muerte anunciada* (1981), as well as in other works, is his carnivalized discourse. Given the pervasiveness of this type of discourse in much of his fiction, it is surprising that it has not received more critical attention, though critics such as Mario Vargas Llosa, Brian J. Mallet, Robert L. Sims, Michael Palencia-Roth, Gene Bell-Villada, and, recently, Isabel Rodríguez-Vergara have studied or commented briefly on this aspect of the Colombian writer's work.[1]

Product of a culture full of vestiges of the Middle Ages, rife with religious dogma and dictatorships that seek to impose the authority of a single, absolute truth on society, García Márquez attempts to undermine "official versions" of reality with his many-voiced narrative fiction (*heteroglossia*, to use Bakhtin's term). Just as Rabelais subverted the "official versions" of his time, helping solidify the humanistic gains of the Renaissance in Europe, employing similar techniques, García Márquez challenges the aesthetic, religious, political, and social dogmas of his culture and time.[2] In view of the pervasive presence of carnivalized discourse in *Cien años*, it is no wonder that Aureliano, who is attempting to decipher Melquíades' manuscript, is attributed the thought, probably reflective of the novelist's view that literature is an excellent toy for making fun of people: "No se le había ocurrido pensar hasta entonces que la literatura fuera el mejor juguete que se había inventado para burlarse de la gente . . ." (327). Rabelais himself could not have said it better. Like Rabelais, García Márquez, through recourse to a multiplicity of voices and with the cleansing effect of laughter, undermines the ready-made values and ideologies society would impose upon its members. Although the Colombian writer evinces a great distrust of theory, the spirit of his writing coincides with the view of the postmodernist theorist Roland Barthes when he wrote in a quintessentially Rabelaisian spirit that the text is "that uninhibited person who shows his behind to the 'Political Father'" (53). Read as a synecdoche, the term "Political Father" can be expanded to include any institutionalized force from the past or the present which attempts to impose its authority on the members of society: Biological Fathers, Church Fathers, Literary Fathers. The chief enemy, whether political, religious, social, or aesthetic, is ideology, which seeks, in Barthes's view, "to 'naturalize' social reality, to make it seem as innocent and unchangeable as nature itself" (Eagleton 136).[3]

García Márquez's carnivalization of his literary world is only one type of discourse he employs, but it is a fundamental element in *Cien años*, and strange as it may seem, since at first glance *Crónica* appears to be much more conventional, it is, albeit less prominent, an important element in this short novel. In some cases there are significant distinctions to be made between García Márquez's carnivalization of discourse and that of Rabelais—as presented by Bakhtin. This is to be expected; although resistance to ideology and authority may originate in a similar human psychology, circumstances change. Some of Bakhtin's ideas can be further illuminated, and even extended, by depth psychology. In García Márquez's narrative one finds certain permutations and commutations, equivalences, and adaptations of the principles employed by Rabelais. After all, it would be quite unRabelaisian for the Colombian novelist to accept *in toto* the "official versions" of Rabelais or Bakhtin! The carnivalization or grotesque realism of discourse has its origins in medieval carnivals and folk celebrations. These celebrations gave license to other types of conduct and voice to other views of reality. The official view and seriousness of the authorities was held up to ridicule and parodied in a variety of ways during folk celebrations. The popular element is also strong in *Cien años* and *Crónica* and indeed in García Márquez's work on the whole. As we shall see, juxtapositions between the popular, folk culture and the official view of various matters contribute significantly to the meanings of the novels.

The "carnivalization of consciousness" reinforced Renaissance values against the decadent but still powerful values of the Middle Ages. Bakhtin provides a lucid account of that clash of values:

> The official culture of the Middle Ages was evolved over many centuries. It had its heroic, creative period and was all embracing and all-penetrating. This culture enveloped and enmeshed the entire world and every segment, even the smallest of human consciousness. It was supported by an organization unique of its kind, the Catholic Church. In the time of the Renaissance the feudal structure was nearing its end, but its ideological domination of the human mind was still extremely powerful.
>
> Where could the Renaissance find support in the struggle against the official culture of the Middle Ages, a struggle which was as intense as it was victorious? The ancient literary sources could not per se offer a sufficient basis because antiquity was also still seen by many through the prism of medieval ideology. In order to discover humanist antiquity, it was necessary at first to be free from the thousand-year domination of medieval categories. It was necessary to gain new ground, to emerge from ideological routine (273-74).

Continuing, Bakhtin affirms that such support was found in folk culture: "Such support could be offered only by the culture of folk humor which had developed through thousands of years" (274). In late twentieth-century Latin America García Márquez and others continue the struggle against what is essentially the dominance of medieval authoritarian values whose sway is strengthened by modern mass-communications techniques and technology. Some of the most effective weapons in the Colombian writer's literary arsenal are the same as those Bakhtin found in Rabelais.

Carnivalized discourse creates a festive public setting and aspires to universality. The reversal of hierarchies, exaggeration, laughter, the fusion of negative and positive characteristics, parody, the leveling of the sacred and the profane, the fusion of the body with the world, the mixing of categories in general, and the presence of polyphonic voices all contribute to the universalization of carnivalized discourse. Writing of the bodily element in the carnivalized consciousness, Bakhtin stresses its public, universal nature:

> It is presented not in a private, egotistic form, severed
> from the other spheres of life, but as something univer-
> sal, representing all the people. As such it is opposed
> to severance from the material and bodily roots of the
> world; it makes no pretence to renunciation of the earth
> or independence of the earth and the body. We repeat:
> the body and the bodily life have here a cosmic and at
> the same time an all-people's character; this is not the
> body and its physiology in the modern sense of the
> words, because it is not individualized. The material
> bodily principle is not contained in the biological indi-
> vidual, not in the bourgeois ego, but in the people, a
> people who are continually growing and renewed. This
> is why all that is bodily becomes grandiose, exagger-
> ated, immeasurable (19).

The presence at the beginning of the novel of Melquíades and his band of gypsies establishes a festive, public tone from the outset. Moreover, the reference to Melquíades' countless trips around the world (12) and the impression he creates of knowing "el otro lado de las cosas" (13), creates about him an aura of universality. The impression he leaves of mastery of the secrets of the universe is not only limited to the present but also includes the past; he is said to possess "las claves de Nostradamus" (13), thus harking back to the past in order to be able to decipher future events.

It goes without saying that examples of the exaggeration that universalize the discourse of *Cien años* are found on every page of the novel. Probably one of the best examples is the description of the return of José Arcadio to Macondo after a long, mysterious absence. His gargantuan proportions, superhuman strength, incredible sexuality, and earth-shaking strides (82-86) place him beyond individuality and transform him into a symbol of universal human forces.

In *Crónica*, for the most part, the carnivalesque elements represent a degradation of the carnivalesque tradition in that the public festivities end in the public sacrifice of an innocent victim. The carnivalesque atmosphere is described early in the novel and initially takes the form of Bayardo San Roman's wedding celebration, which soon turns into a public affair that includes everyone in the community. After a description of the prodigal provisions for the wedding celebration, the narrator attests to its public nature: "No hubo una sola persona, ni pobre ni rica, que no hubiera participado de algún modo en la parranda de mayor escándalo que se había visto jamás en el pueblo" (28). The public nature of the wedding is again emphasized when the narrator says that it developed its own momentum causing Bayardo San Román to lose control of it: " . . . [L]a Fiesta adquirió una fuerza propia tan difícil de amaestrar, que al mismo Bayardo San Román se le salió de las manos y terminó por ser un acontecimiento público" (54). Yet again, the narrator refers to the public nature of the celebration, saying that it disperses, but continues, around midnight: "La parranda pública se dispersó en fragmentos hacia la media noche . . ." (62).

The dispersal of the public in small groups is, nevertheless, temporary. The murder of Santiago Nasar brings the town people together again early the following morning. Virtually everyone knows about the Vicario twins threat, and virtually everyone is present at the town square to witness the crime. Several passages stress the public nature of the event:

> La gente se dispersaba hacia la plaza en el mismo sentido que ellos [Santiago Nasar and Cristo Bedoya] (134).

> . . . [L]a gente sabía que Santiago Nasar iba a morir, y no se atrevía a tocarlo (134).

> La gente que regresaba del puerto, alertada por los gritos, empezó a tomar posiciones en la plaza para presenciar el crimen (142).

> La gente se había situado en la plaza como en los días de desfiles (149).

> [Pedro and Pablo Vicario] no oyeron los gritos del pueblo entero espantado de su propio crimen (153).

The carnivalesque tradition manifests itself in a degraded form in *Crónica* because what begins as a liberating, festive occasion in which the whole town participates winds up as a ritual human sacrifice, though years later there is a kind of displaced renewal in the case of Angela Vicario, of which more later. What force intervenes to deflect the carnival spirit of the wedding celebration onto a destructive path? The carnivalesque spirit of gaiety and the celebration of the body collide with the townspeople's adherence to a decadent code of honor based on the cult of virginity, which in turn derives from a narrow

Catholic morality savoring the mortification of the flesh. Needless to say, perhaps, the cult of virginity is based on a double
standard for men and women. The carnivalesque tradition is
degraded here because of the failure to integrate higher and
lower human functions. From the standpoint of psychoanalysis,
this is tantamount to a failure to integrate ego, id, and superego
functions. The carnival tradition is degraded here because of the
failure to integrate higher and lower human functions. From
the standpoint of psychoanalysis, this is tantamount to a failure
to integrate ego, id, and superego functions. The carnival gaiety
which in this case is largely an unconscious function of the id,
and the adherence to the decadent code of honor, which is
largely conscious and occupies too little space in the townspeople's psychic functioning.

   In García Márquez, as in Rabelais, there occurs a suspen-
sion or reversal of official hierarchies. Writing of the medieval
festive events, Bakhtin describes the nature of these reversals:

> The usual order and way of life and especially the so-
> cial hierarchy were suspended at the wedding feast.
> Rules of politeness among equals and of respect for the
> hierarchy among inferiors were cancelled for that short
> period. Conventions banished, the distance between
> men disappeared, and all this was symbolically ex-
> pressed by the right to strike one's important and es-
> teemed neighbor. During the short time of the wedding
> feast all participants entered, as it were, the utopian
> kingdom of absolute equality and freedom (264).

   In *Cien años* and *Crónica* the carnivalesque takes the form
of a challenge of ready-made values, a rejection of absolutes, pu-
rities, rationalism, stereotypes, and dogmas. It evinces a more
than healthy skepticism of official truths. Also, it displays a constant distrust of theory and a blurring of boundaries between the
categories which all too often channel thinking. This is evident
from the outset in the "magical realism" of *Cien años* where the
ordinary distinctions between a realist and a "magical" style are
blurred and in *Crónica* where we find a rare mixture of discourses associated with journalism and detective fiction, producing symbolic resonances that go far beyond expectation for either
of these types of discourse. In general, it seems fair to say that
García Márquez's writing is animated by the desire to assert the
claims of the body (instinctual life) against the demands of society in order to achieve, as in the case of Rabelais, a superior inte-

gration of these two sets of claims. In *Desire in Language,* Julia Kristeva, whose theory of intertextuality derives in part from Bakhtin's theories of carnivalization and dialogism, uses the word "rhythm" to refer to the force that moves the writer to re-make language in his or her own image: "The poet is put to death because he wants to turn rhythm into a dominant element; because he wants to make language perceive what it doesn't want to say, provide it with its matter independently of the sign, and free it from denotation. For it is this *eminently parodic* gesture that changes the system" (31). Roland Barthes asserts that original writers reject denotation or fixed meanings and abstractions, and he uses the metaphor "names" for unoriginal, static language:

> . . . [T]he text *does not give names*—or it removes existing ones; it does not say (or with what *dubious* intent?): Marxism, Brechtism, capitalism, idealism, Zen, etc.; the Name does not cross its lips, it is fragmented into practices, into word which are not Names. Bringing itself to the limits of speech, in a *mathesis* of language which does not seek to be identified with science, the text undoes nomination, and it is this defection which approaches bliss (45).

The mixing of categories, the binary oppositions, and the polyphonic elements contributing to the carnivalesque discourse of *Cien años* and *Crónica* compose a list almost too lengthy to enumerate: sexual purity and modesty vs. prostitution and free love, life vs. death, the official version vs. the empirical version, history vs. literature, liberals vs. conservatives, the fusion of past, present, and future times, pagan vs. Christian values, the sacred vs. the profane, the conscious vs. the unconscious, the private vs. the public, the serious vs. the comic.

What Bakhtin terms the "bodily principle" plays an important role in García Márquez, as it does in Rabelais, and in the Colombian writer's fiction, as in that of his predecessor, such images are often exaggerated. Bakhtin writes: ". . . [I]n Rabelais' work the material bodily principle, that is, images of the human body with its food, drink, defecation, and sexual life, plays a dominant role" (18). He continues, stressing the positive, universal, and integrative import of the bodily principle:

> In grotesque realism, therefore, the bodily element is deeply positive. It is presented not in a private ego-

tistic form, severed from the other spheres of life, but
as something universal, representing all the people. As
such it is opposed to severance from the bodily roots of
the world; it makes no pretense to renunciation of the
earth or independence of the earth and the body (19).

What Bakhtin calls the bodily principle, emphasis on the
cloacal or lower body functions, is prominent in both *Cien años*
and *Crónica*; in some instances this principle also exemplifies
the reversal of hierarchies. García Márquez's "bad women,"
whose functioning in society revolves around the bodily pleasure they provide are uniformly associated not only with sexual
gratification but also tenderness, generosity, empathy, consolation, and fertility. In *Cien años* one only has to think of Pilar
Ternera, who even in her old age, like La Celestina, takes pleasure in the knowledge of other people's sexual fulfillment: "Soy
feliz sabiendo que la gente es feliz en la cama" (135). Then there
is Petra Cotes whose relations with Aureliano Segundo result
not only in the multiplication of his herd of cattle but also become the catalyst for a positive transformation of his personality:

> La naturaleza lo había hecho reservado y esquivo, con
> tendencias a la meditación solitaria y ella le había
> moldeado el carácter opuesto, vital, expansivo,
> desabrochado y le había infundido el júbilo de vivir y
> el placer de la parranda y el despilfarro hasta conver-
> tirlo, por dentro y por fuera, en el hombre con que había
> soñado desde la adolescencia (177).

In *Crónica* it is María Alejandrina Cervantes who epitomizes this reversal of hierarchies involving the bodily principle.
While the rest of the town, animated and legitimized by their
cult of virginity, collaborates in the murder and dismemberment
of Santiago Nasar, María Alejandrina Cervantes, along with her
mulattoes, teaches the young man of the town the value of love
and tenderness. Overcome with inconsolable grief when she
learns of Santiago's death, she closes her establishment in
mourning. The narrator's use of the word "apostólico" to describe María Alejandrina underscores the primacy, the sacred-
ness, if you will, of the body in the novel's implicit hierarchy of
values, just the opposite, of course, of the place given to the body
in the Church doctrine underlying the townspeople's action.[4]
The narrator explains that when he heard the tolling of the
church bells announcing Santiago's death, he was recovering

from the wedding party "en el regazo apostólico de María Alejandrina" (11).

The primacy of the body is further emphasized in *Crónica* when the narrator evokes the image of the completely naked María Alejandrina trying to console herself by eating enormous amounts of food:

> Encontré a María Alejandrina Cervantes despierta como siempre al amanecer, y desnuda por completo como siempre que no había extraños en la casa. Estaba sentada a la turca sobre la cama de reina frente a un platón babilónico do cosas de comer; costillas de ternera, una gallina hervida, lomo de cerdo, y una guarnición de plátanos y legumbres que hubieran alcanzado para cinco. Comer sin medida fue siempre su único modo de llorar, y nunca la había visto hacerlo con semejante pesadumbre (101-02).

That María Alejandrina exemplifies the primacy of the body is further stressed here by her attempt to assuage her grief through the bodily function of eating.

The reversal of hierarchies, in which prostitutes and mistresses reign supreme, took place, according to Bakhtin, on May Day eve: "Fairies protect prostitutes, who also reign supreme on May Day even with its license and revelry. Dame Douce and the fairies represent the unofficial world, which that night is granted full liberty and impunity" (259).

The positive value of García Márquez's "bad women" is heightened by the juxtaposition with his "good women." A highly satirical presentation in *Cien años* of women like Amaranta and Fernanda, who represent puritanical values, is sustained throughout the novel. The presentation of Remedios, la bella, further contributes, in my judgment, to this satirical picture. As I have suggested above, in *Crónica* the town's cult of virginity is the novel's principal target of criticism.

Unconscionably, Amaranta successively encourages and rejects two suitors, Pietro Crespi and Colonel Gerineldo Márquez, causing the former to commit suicide and cutting off the latter in an abusive and cruel fashion. Having burned her matrimonial bridges in this manner, she then involves her young nephews in endless and exhausting incestuous play, which is never consummated in a full sexual act. Technically, then, Amaranta remains a virgin, and it is this idea which, despite her cruelty to her suitors and what amounted to sexual "foreplay" with her young nephews, gives meaning to her at the end of her life. She sews her own shroud, lies down to die at the time she had announced and demands that Ursula publicly certify that she dies a virgin. Ursula, ignorant of her incestuous activity, immediately assents to do so: "Amaranta Buendía se va de este mundo como vino" (240). Symbolically, Amaranta's shroud is a womb. Ursula's words ironically suggest that Amaranta, out of her fear of life, has really never lived, has never left the womb. Amaranta's hypocrisy is transparent. Not only has her overvaluation of virginity led to a life of sterility but she has manifestly harmed those around her. Traditionally treated as a symbol of purity, innocence and virtue, virginity metamorphoses in this context into a symbol of sterility and death.[5]

The demythologization of virginity is reinforced by Fernanda's puritanism, which is evident in her aversion to sex, bodily functions, and the ordinary language used to refer to these functions. Even Amaranta makes fun of Fernanda's euphemisms: "*Esfetafa*—decía—*esfe defe lasfa quefe lesfe tifiefenenfe asfa cofo ofa sufu profopifiafa mifierfedafa*" (183). Brought up by her parents to believe that she was destined to be a queen, Fernanda takes pride in considering that she is the only person in the region

> . . . de no haber hecho del cuerpo sino en bacinillas de oro, para que luego el coronel Aureliano Buendía, que en paz descanse, tuviera el atrevimiento de preguntar con mala bilis de masón de dónde había merecido ese privilegio, si era que ella no cagaba mierda, sino astromelias, imagínese, con esas palabras, y para que Renata, su propia hija, que por indiscreción había visto sus aguas mayores en el dormitorio, contestara que de verdad la bacinilla era de mucho oro y de mucha heráldica, pero que lo que tenía dentro era pura mierda, mierda física, y peor todavía que las otras porque era mierda de cachaca . . ." (275).

All this echoes the exchanges between don Quijote and Sancho over the "yelmo de Mambrino" or, as Sancho is finally intimidated into calling it, the "baciyelmo." This passage reveals, then, an attack on Hispanic puritanism, quixotic idealism, and pretensions to nobility.

Fernanda's puritanical attitude inevitably translates into actions destructive of others. When she learns that her daughter

Meme is meeting Mauricio Babilonia every night, on the pretext that a chicken thief has been stealing chickens she hires a night watchman who shoots the hapless lover, leaving him bedridden the rest of his life (248). Later, when Meme gives birth to a child, Fernanda, fearful of a scandal, cannot bring herself to drown the child in the bathtub so she brings him out of hiding, but only after it occurs to her to persuade others that she found him floating in a basket (249). But for Fernanda this is not enough; in order to "eliminar todo vestigio del oprobio" (248), and without consulting with her husband, she packs Meme's bag with three changes of clothes and sends her off to a dark hospital in Krakow where she spends the rest of her life (249-52).

Much has been written about the significance of Remedios, la bella. In an interview with Gabriele Morelli, the novelist himself suggested that this character does not quite fit into the novel: "Remedios la bella, è un persaggio non ben delineato nel senso che non appartiene completamente a *Cent'anni de solitudine*; anzi è un poco come si fosse di un altro libro; non ha il carattere del Buendía" (125). For Benjamín Torres, Remedios, la bella, represents "la boda sagrada o espiritual entre cielo y tierra" (194). Although it may be true, as García Márquez says, that Remedios, la bella's personality is unlike that of the other Buendías, in my judgment, she does contribute significantly to an important theme in the novel. She is a parody, a *reductio ad aburdum* of the ideal of sexual purity in human conduct. She is the Virgin Mary resurrected, made flesh, and living among men. Although Remedios, la bella, is beautiful and extremely attractive to men, she is unable to understand and feel what they feel. Her purity and innocence not only make her indifferent to normal relations between men and women, but she is also unable to perform even the simplest domestic chores. Moreover, she is unmalicious femme fatale, leaving a wake of destroyed men in her path. Remedios, la bella, then, in my view, symbolizes the sterility of the concept of purity as a model for human conduct. Worse, she actually inflicts harm, albeit unconsciously (170ff), on others. For these reasons it is difficult to agree with Torres that she represents a union between heaven and earth. The unintentional nature of the harm that Remedios, la bella, does has a parallel in the harm done by the mindless inertia of the devotees of the Church's cult of virginity. She really is not of the earth. Thematically, the presentation of Remedias, la bella, reinforces the implicit attack in *Cien años* on the notion of purity in human affairs, also satirized in the presentations of Amaranta and Fernanda.

Certain episodes exemplify multiple elements of carnivalesque discourse. In his *García Márquez: historia de un deicidio,* Vargas Llosa has documented the Rabelaisian exaggeration, "la descomunalidad," a general feature of García Márquez's style in *Cien años* (170-71), which José Arcadio exemplifies with his enormous size and feats of physical strength. He arrives like an earthquake, shaking the house to its foundation, performs incredible feats of strength, and displays his gigantic body covered with tattoos, souvenirs of his seventy-five trips around the globe. Women are fascinated with the size of his tattooed phallus, and he raffles himself off at ten pesos a number (84). His eating feats are no less gargantuan: ". . . [S]e comía medio lechón en el almuerzo," and, true to his Rabelaisian forebears, he does not deign to suppress disgusting bodily habits, including "ventosidades que marchitaban las flores" and "eructos bestiales" that repelled his family (85).

When José Arcadio tells Pietro Crespi that he is going to marry Rebeca, Pietro turns pale and tells the giant that since Rebeca is his sister (adoptive), such an act is both against the law and against nature. José Arcadio's reply is vintage carnivalesque: "Me cago dos veces en natura . . ." (86). The consummation of the marriage is a scandalous, public affair: "Los vecinos se asustaban con los gritos que despertaban a todo el barrio hasta ocho veces en una noche, y hasta tres veces en la siesta, y rogaban que una pasión tan desaforada no fuera a perturbar la paz de los muertos" (86).

Partly because of the hyperbolic language used in these episodes the carnivalesque bodily principle is prominent here; the emphasis on sexual activity, the exaggerated appetite, the farts, the eructations, and the reference to defecating on nature. Two other important carnivalesque elements are present: the public nature of all that José Arcadio does, including his publicly audible honeymoon and the universalization of his mode of being. The larger-than-life quality of his body and all that he does mean that he is not just an individual but a symbol of irrepressible vital forces operating in humanity throughout the world and across the centuries. His sexual prowess, reflecting his status as a "protomacho" make him a symbol of the irrepressible sexuality of the species. The semipublic nature of his honeymoon reinforces the collective, or better, the universal nature of the force. José Arcadio dramatizes the exuberant vitality of human beings, which has its origins in the body. In the beginning was the body. . . .

The presence of the bodily principle is also evident in Ursula's fear of producing an offspring with a pig's tail and the fulfillment of that fear at the end of the novel when Aureliano and Amaranta Ursula's incestuous love produces a child with a pig's tail, the last member of the family, who is devoured by ants. Another episode, too frequently noted as Rabelaisian in nature, to merit further comment, is the eating contest between Aureliano Segundo and Camila Sagastume, "La Elefanta" (220-21).

In *Crónica* the bodily principle manifests itself in a less straightforward and more complex manner than in *Cien años*. Moreover, it rarely provokes the laughter usually associated with its presence in *Cien años*, though in some cases it may give rise to a sort of black humor. Here the bodily principle is related to the disparity between the characters' conscious and unconscious psychology. Also, it is related to the carnivalesque elements of the reversal of hierarchies, parody, degradation, and, indirectly, renewal through the integration of body and soul or of lower and higher processes.

As I have argued elsewhere ("The Sleep of Vital Reason . . ."), the role of the body in human conduct is a central theme in *Crónica*. True to the carnival spirit, the novel implicitly advocates the primacy of bodily functions, censuring the cult of virginity and the undervaluation of corporal needs. All the references to the body function within the framework of this thematic focus, though certain elements also play an anticipatory role in the novel.

Such is the case when Santiago Nasar enters the kitchen to eat breakfast where Victoria Guzmán is preparing three rabbits for lunch. Irritated by his pursuit of her daughter Divina Flor, whom he has just grabbed by the wrist and threatened: "Ya estás en tiempo de desbravar" (17), she pointedly shows him her bloodied knife, ordering him to let go of her daughter. Victoria then tells Santiago: "De esta agua no beberás mientras yo esté viva" (17). And just to spoil his breakfast, "[Victoria] arrancó de cuajo las entrañas un conejo y les tiró a los perros el tripajo humeante" (18). Santiago's reaction and the presence of the dogs betray the incident's anticipatory nature: "No seas bárbara—le dijo él—. Imagínate que fuera un ser humano" (18). What is anticipated, of course, is the murder of Santiago and the excitement these same dogs show aroused by the smell of the protruding intestines.

The murder of Santiago and the mutilation of his body have their origins both in the carnivalesque tradition and the Church's aversion to the body. Santiago is a Christ figure whose murder and mutilation are the end-products of the Church's cult of virginity upon which the town's code of honor is based. The carnivalesque tradition announces its presence both in the degradation occasioned by the brutal form of the murder and in the mutilation of Santiago's body during the autopsy. Degradation, according to Bakhtin, is the essential principle of carnivalesque discourse:

> The essential principle of grotesque realism is degradation, that is, the lowering of all that is high, spiritual, ideal, abstract: it is a transfer to the material level, to the sphere of earth and body in their indissoluble unity (19-20).

As for dismemberment and mutilation, Bakhtin affirms that oaths and swearing are a symbolic tearing apart of the human body and that, for the most part, this symbolized a rending of the Lord's body:

> What is the thematic content of the oaths? It is mainly the rending of the human body. Swearing was mostly done in the name of the members and the organs of the divine body: the Lord's body, the head, blood, wounds, bowels; or in the name of the relics of saints and martyrs—feet, hands, fingers—which were preserved in churches (192).

Bakhtin continues: "The dismembered body and its anatomization play a considerable part in Rabelais' novel" (193). It is important to remember that the ultimate goal is an integration of lower and higher functions to form an "indissoluble unity."

Just as *Don Quixote* degrades chivalry, *Crónica* degrades the Church's enthronement of chastity as an ideal for human life. Perhaps the earliest clue to this interpretation is the recounting early in the novel of the incident in which a maid accidentally discharges a pistol that destroys a life-size plaster saint on the main altar of the church. As we shall see later, though Santiago himself is not resurrected, there is a displaced resurrection, rebirth or renewal in Angela Vicario's awakening to autonomy at the end of the novel.

The murder of Santiago by two hog butchers with crude, rusty knives with which they "nail" him to the wooden door of his own house parodies the crucification of Christ. The stigma-like wound in his hand further contributes to the parody. The detailed description of one of the bloodiest and most hair-raising murders ever rendered in literature has nothing gratuitous about it, but rather is a dramatic *reductio ad absurdum* of the Church's doctrine of the mortification of the flesh. The parody and degradation converge in the description of the autopsy Father Carmen Amador performs on Santiago's body. Of the autopsy the narrator exclaims: "Fue un masacre" (98). He continues:

> Nos devolvieron un cuerpo distinto. La mitad del cráneo había sido destrozada con la trepanación, y el rostro del galán que la muerte había preservado acabó de perder su identidad. Además, el párroco había arrancado de cuajo las vísceras destazadas, pero al final no supo qué hacer con ellos, y les impartió una bendición de rabia y las tiró en el balde de la basura" (100).

Notice the similarity of the language, "había arrancado de cuajo," to that used to describe Victoria Guzmán's dressing of the rabbits.

The townspeople's adherence to a code of honor that, in the last analysis, denies the claims of the body presupposes an excessive disparity between their conscious and unconscious psychology and the failure to effect a functional synthesis (similar to what Ortega called "vital reason") between the two layers of their psyches. The result is the death of Santiago. The role the unconscious plays in their conduct is most dramatically exemplified in the psychosomatic symptoms the Vicario twins exhibit after they are incarcerated. Moreover, their announcing of their intentions of committing the murder suggests that at least unconsciously they wished to be stopped. Consciously, they feel no remorse; in the three years they awaited trial "nunca advirtieron en ellos ningún indicio de arrepentimiento" (67). Nevertheless, they do repent; at least their bodies repent. They cannot sleep without reenacting the nightmare of the murder (103), and they are unable to rid themselves of the smell of Santiago's body (103, 104). Recalling their incarceration, Pedro exclaims: "Estuve despierto once meses" (105). Even though their food is prepared by their mother, Pablo develops "una colerina pestilente," which convinces Pedro that someone has poisoned his brother (105). Pedro Vicario is unable to urinate and Pablo cannot stop urinating. The Vicario twins and the townspeople alike feared an attempt at revenge by the Arabic community, to which Santiago belonged on his father's side. In reality, however, their fears are groundless; the Arabic community is peaceful and not at all interested in revenge. Significantly, the brothers' symptoms disappear when they take a concoction recommended by the Arabic matriarch Suseme Abdala:

> Más aún: fue Suseme Abdala, la matriarca centenaria, quien reommendó la infusión prodigiosa de flores de pasionaria y ajenjo mayor que segó la colerina de Pablo Vicario y desató a la vez el manantial florido de su gemelo. Pedro Vicario cayó entonces en un sopor insomne, y el hermano restablecido concilió su primer sueño sin remordimientos (108).

Suseme Abdala's cure is a gesture of forgiveness which relieves the consciences of the twins and rids them of their unconscious guilt feelings. Consciously, they accept the widely-accepted belief that the murder was justified in order to avenge the family's sullied honor, but on a deeper level, a better, humane unideological human self is revulsed at what they have done. It is this deeper, unconscious self that makes them announce their intentions in hopes of being stopped, and it is this self that gives rise to the host of symptoms that afflict them in jail.

The solution to the problem of unconsciously-motivated conduct (the superego in this case) lies in becoming aware of a deeper level of the unconscious—in paying attention to the symptoms originating from this level. The twins' symptoms suggest that the cure lies in heeding the claims of the body, in this case a deeper, wholesome, more humane revulsion to the atrocity they have committed. What is lacking is an integration of higher and lower functions (id, ego, and superego) in their conduct and in the "ideology" of the townspeople. The novel leads the reader to perceive this need, but the characters themselves do not become aware of it. Such an integration is the goal of carnivalized discourse, and in this case, the novelist's working knowledge of depth psychology gives new meaning to the process of integration.

Opposed to the Christian mortification of the flesh in *Crónica* is a pagan glorification of the body. This reversal of the usual Christian-pagan opposition, in which "pagan" is the pejorative term, is achieved in many ways, but the key to understanding the reversal is the Xius story. His name is probably a corruption of "Zeus"; like Zeus, he lives high on a hill with an Olympic view. His home, with its many happy memories, is taken over by the quintessential Christian Bayardo San Román. The novel seems to be a dramatization of Nietzsche's judgment: "Christianity gave Eros poison to drink; he did not die of it, certainly, but degenerated to Vice" (90).

Another aspect of carnivalized discourse in *Cien años* and *Crónica* is the transformation of identities brought about through the use of masks and ritualized role-playing. In Bakhtin's view the wearing of masks has several implications:

> The mask is connected with the joy of change and reincarnations, with gay relativity and the merry negation of uniformity and similarity; it rejects conformity to oneself. The mask is related to transition, metamorphoses, the violation of natural boundaries, to mockery and familiar nicknames. It contains the playful element of life. . . . Let us point out that such manifestations as parodies, caricatures, grimaces, eccentric postures, and comic gestures are per se derived from the mask. It reveals the essence of the grotesque (39-40).

During a carnival celebration Aureliano Segundo disguises himself as a tiger: "El carnaval había alcanzado su más alto nivel de locura, Aureliano Segundo había satisfecho por fin su sueño de disfrazarse de tigre y andaba feliz entre la muchedumbre desaforado, ronco de tanto roncar . . ." (174). It is evident that the other celebrants of Macondo also wore masks when they are described as removing them to get a better look at the dazzling figure of Fernanda del Carpio. Fernanda makes her first appearance in Macondo dressed as a queen, "con corona de esmeraldas y capa de armiño, que parecía investido de una autoridad legítima, y no simplemente de una soberanía de lentejuelas y papel crespón" (175). Fernanda's regal presence derives not only from her extraordinary beauty but also from having been reared by her parents to believe that she was destined to be queen. Aureliano Segundo places the intruding queen on the same pedestal as Remedios, la bella, the local carnival queen. This carnivalesque episode in particular and the overall presen-

tation of Fernanda make fun of and parody the impractical, pre-
tentious, and quixotic upbringing of which so many Hispanic
women have been victims.

The mask element appears in *Crónica* in Santiago Nasar's
relations with María Alejandrina Cervantes and her mulattoes.
Santiago is said to possess an extraordinary ability for disguising
the mulattoes:

> Santiago Nasar tenía un talento casi mágico para
> los disfraces, y su diversión predilecta era trastrocar la
> identidad de las mulatas. Saqueaba los roperos de unas
> para disfrazar a las otras, de modo que terminaban por
> sentirse distintas de sí mismas e iguales a las que no
> eran. En cierta ocasión, una de ellas se vio repetida en
> otra con tal acierto, que sufrió una crisis de llanto.
> "Sentí que me había salido del espejo," dijo (87-88).

This incident is a hint to the reader on how to read this novel
and perhaps novels in general. Just as Santiago, alters, confuses,
and erases the boundaries between identities, so does the novelist disguise his intertexts through displacement, condensation,
irony, metaphor, and metonomy. In his interview with Plinio
Apuleyo Mendoza, the novelist asserted that "una novela es una
representación cifrada de la realidad, una especie de adivinanza
del mundo" (48), which is tantamount to saying that the novel is
an unmasked version of reality. This is not far from saying that
the novel, at least as García Márquez defines it, is a carnivalization of reality, whose function it is to challenge and subvert established or official realities.

Renewal or rebirth is a key characteristic of carnivalesque
discourse. According to Bakhtin, such discourse entails the presentation of a positive, dynamic process:

> The last thing one can say of the real grotesque is that
> it is static; on the contrary, it seeks to grasp in its im-
> agery the very act of becoming and growth, the com-
> plete unfinished nature of being. Its images present
> simultaneously the two poles of becoming: that which
> is receding and dying, and that which is being born;
> they show two bodies in one, the budding and division
> of the living cell (52).

Such a renewal or rebirth is present in *Cien años* precisely
because of its conspicuous absence. In the last analysis, renewal

manifests itself in a negative fashion. It is true, of course, that in the history of the Buendía family there are flashes of renewal, usually associated with sexual vitality, which, as we have seen, symbolizes positive growth, fertility, and the fullness of life. The novel chronicles innumerable repetitions, but the repetitions themselves reveal a waning vitality. It is Pilar Ternera, one of the good "bad women" who perceives most clearly the trajectory of the Buendía clan:

> No había ningún misterio en el corazón de un Buendía, que fuera impenetrable para ella, proque un siglo de naipes y de experiencia le había enseñado que la historia de la familia era un engranaje de repeticiones irreparables, una rueda giratoria que hubiera seguido dando vueltas hasta la eternidad, do no haber sido por el desgaste progresivo e irremediable del eje (334).

The general decline of the Buendía family overwhelms the flashes of insight and renewal that too infrequently occur in the lives of the Buendías. The family's failure to renew itself is related, in part, to their failure to integrate the higher and lower levels of their functioning; the conscious and the unconscious, the corporal and the spiritual, the Dionysian and the Apollonian, vitality and reason. Although Ursula is possessed of a strong will, good judgment, common sense, and, paradoxically, as she gradually loses her sight, clairvoyance, she too, albeit on a lesser scale, represents the old, puritanical order that tends to reject change and the claims of the body. Moreover, she alone is unable to slow the mindless impetus of the Buendía physical vitality. Positive vitality also manifests itself in the inventiveness of José Arcadio Buendía. Yet his scientific discoveries, or rediscoveries, reveal the cultural isolation of Macondo. Also, Petra Cotes and Pilar Ternera exemplify the bodily principle in a positive fashion, but without any particular integration with spiritual or Apollonian functions.

Integration and renewal occur in a displaced form in *Crónica*. Angela Vicario is coerced by her family, and especially by her mother Pura del Carmen, into marrying a man she does not love. However, despite Bayardo San Roman's rejection of her when he discovers that she is not a virgin, she ultimately falls in love with him. But this occurs only after she is "reborn." Her rebirth takes the form of a sudden recognition of the petty vanities of her mother, who had always dominated her life. Not only had Pura forced her into a marriage without love, but after her rejection by Bayardo, "había hecho más que lo posible para que Angela se muriera en vida" (117). Earlier, the narrator had said that Pura "había tratado de enterrarla en vida" (115). Angela's awakening gives her the strength to sever the bonds that enslave her to her mother's will. She becomes an autonomous human being. In true carnivalesque fashion the images of burial and rebirth are juxtaposed to encompass a larger human process.

Psychological integration takes places in that she is no longer caught between her deepest desires and the desire to please her mother. Immediately following her rebirth she falls madly in love with Bayardo San Román: "Nació de nuevo. 'Me volví loca por él—me dijo—, loca de remate (121). From this moment, she begins writing the nearly two thousand letters which Bayardo does not answer and eventually returns to her in person unopened.

Angela's "burial" and her disinterment or psychological rebirth conform almost perfectly to the carnivalized discourse described by Bakhtin:

> Degradation digs a bodily grave for a new birth; it has not only a destructive, negative aspect, but also a regenerating one. To degrade an object does not imply merely hurling it into absolute destruction, but to hurl it down to the reproductive lower stratum, the zone in which conception and a new birth take place. Grotesque realism knows no other level; it is the fruitful earth and womb. It is always conceiving (21).

The carnivalization of discourse then is a means of representing the dynamic nature of life, the fusion of what initially appear as opposing forces in human affairs and the lives of individuals, the renewal and rebirth that develop out of degradation.

Carnivalized discourse, as Bakhtin conceives it, is not just limited to the integration of the lower and the higher, but also of a fusion of other categories in order to achieve a more balanced and complete picture of what it means to be human: "The grotesque symposium does not have to respect hierarchical distinctions; it freely blends the profane and the sacred, the lower and the higher, the spiritual and the material" (286). Later, he adds that such discourse exploits "the possibility of combining in one image the positive and the negative phase." García Márquez evinces a masterly ability to blend and fuse polar oppositions and diverse categories, as well as to dissipate stereotypes and conventional expectations. The magical realism of *Cien años* is a major example of the synthesis of almost innumerable types of discourse; magical, mythological, biblical, chivalric, realist, surrealist, historical, biographical. In this respect he has achieved a synthesis of types of discourses in our time comparable to the synthesis Cervantes achieved in his time with *Don Quixote*. But this is a complex matter that has been dealt with extensively by other critics which need not be repeated or belabored here.[6]

Although many critics have commented on Melquíades seemingly easy passage between life and death (49, 67, 124, 161), there are other less obvious cases of the fusion of life and death in a single image. The description of Prudencio Aguilar's periodic "return to life" corresponds to the guilt feelings that overwhelm José Arcadio and Ursula. Nevertheless, the scenes are presented ambiguously, as a vision, a hallucination, or even as reality:

> El asunto fue clasificado como un duelo de honor, pero a ambos les quedó un molestar en la conciencia. Una noche en que no podía dormir, Ursula salió a tomar agua en el patio y vio a Prudencio Aguilar junto a la tinaja. Estaba lívido con una expresión muy triste (26).

Ursula tells José Arcadio that "los muertos no salen . . ." (26). Continuing, she says: "Lo que pasa es que no podemos con la conciencia" (26). However, both Ursula and José Arcadio continue seeing Prudencio until they leave to establish Macondo. Later, when José Arcadio is tied under the chestnut tree he talks with Prudencio twice a day (124).

Ursula's demise confuses the boundaries between life and death. Hearing the other members of her family jokingly insist that she has died, she yields to the evidence, actually dying two days later:

> —Pobre la tatarabuelita—dijo Amaranta Ursula— se nos murió de vieja.
> Ursula se sobresaltó.
> —¡Estoy viva!—dijo.
> —Ya ves—dijo Amaranta Ursula, reprimiendo la risa—, ni siquiera respira.
> —¡Estoy hablando!—gritó Ursula.
> —Ni siquiera habla—dijo Aureliano—Se murió como un grillito.

> Entonces Ursula se rindió a la evidencia. "Dios
> mío," exclamó en voz baja. "De modo que esto es la
> muerte" (290).

Ursula's passage from life to death presupposes a mixture of objective and subjective elements in both life and death. The meaning of both words is fixed socially. To a large extent we are defined by others through our common language. When Ursula dies she is the size of a baby, small enough to be placed in a basket the size of the one in which Aureliano was "found" (291). This image suggests that her death is a kind of birth or rebirth. Another such image is the shroud Amaranta sews in anticipation of her death. The shroud resembles the womb to which the virginal Amaranta returns without having had the courage to love or, symbolically, to live. The cases of Meme, who Fernanda buries in life in a convent in Krakow, and Angela Vicario, in *Crónica*, whose mother did all she could to bury her in life (115, 117), have already been discussed. The rattling bones of Rebeca's parents are another single image of life and death (171). Rebeca also buries herself in life after José Arcadio's death. When Ursula dies, Amaranta Ursula fails in her vigorous efforts to restore order and life to the home because of Fernanda's determination to bury herself in life:

> La pasión claustral de Fernanda puso un dique infran-
> queable a los cien años torrenciales de Ursula. No sólo
> se negó el viento árido, sino que hizo clausurar las ven-
> tanas con crucetas de madera, obedeciendo a la consigna
> paterna de enterrarse en vida (294).

The distinction between the labels liberal and conservative is ultimately blurred into indistinction in *Cien años*. Initially, it appears that the liberals, represented by Colonel Aureliano Buendía and his associates, take up arms to combat the efforts of the central government to control Macondo and to fight for justice. Eventually, however, it becomes evident that each side fights out of pride, the desire for self-aggrandizement, and sheer love of power.

When the church tower is destroyed by conservatives and rebuilt by liberals, Father Nicanor is perplexed: "Esto es un disparate: los defensores de la fe de Cristo destruyen el templo y los masones lo mandan componer" (119). In a conversation with his comrade-in-arms Colonel Gerineldo Márquez, Colonel Aure-

liano Buendía exclaims: "Yo, por mi parte, apenas ahora me doy
cuenta que estoy peleando por orgullo" (121). Recapturing Macondo from the conservatives, Colonel Aureliano Buendía is
revealed to be no less arrogant and despotic than were the conservatives (138ff). During the time of the banana fever Colonel
Aureliano Buendía observes: "La única diferencia actual entre
liberales y conservadores, es que los liberales van a misa de cinco
y los conservadores van a misa de ocho" (209).

The effect of virtually erasing the distinction between liberals and conservatives is to diminish the fundamental importance of ideology in human motivation, which all too often jus-
tifies and enmasks plain old self-seeking and pride. The labels
which attach themselves to human beings are often accidents of
time and place of birth or other adventitious circumstances. The
novel strips away the ideological pretensions of the characters
and the stereotypical expectations of the readers, leaving bare the
human striving underneath.

The artificiality, arbitrariness, and inadequacy of human
labels also become evident with regard to time, which possesses
a large subjective element. Observing on a certain Tuesday that
nothing has changed, José Arcadio Buendía complains that it
continues to be Monday: "'Pero de pronto me he dado cuenta de
que sigue siendo lunes, como ayer. Mira el cielo, mira las paredes, mira las begonias. También hoy es lunes'" (73). Later, he
exclaims, almost sobbing: "'¡La máquina del tiempo se ha des-
compuesto . . .'" (73). Notwithstanding these outbursts being
considered as symptoms of insanity which lead to José Arcadio
Buendía's being tethered beneath the chestnut tree, the hapless
inventor's departure from the reality of common sense is based
on a sound understanding of the nature of language. As in the
Borges's story "Funes el memorioso," José Arcadio Buendía's
observation presupposes that signs should be based on distinguishable differences. His insight further reminds the reader
that the boundaries between sanity and insanity are far from easy
to fix. Remember that José Arcadio Buendía's "insanity" was anticipated by his "insane" discovery that the world is round.

In her extreme old age Ursula gradually begins to confuse
the present with the past, conversing with long dead relatives:
" . . . [P]oco a poco fue perdiendo el sentido de la realidad, y confundía el tiempo actual con épocas remotas de su vida, hasta el
punto de que en una ocasión pasó tres días llorando sin consuelo
por la muerte de Petronila Iguarán, su bisabuela, enterrada desde

hacía más de un siglo" (277-78). José Arcadio Segundo's repeti-
tion of an old saying of Ursula's about the passing of time provokes a recognition on her part that the statement is really not
true:

> Al decirlo, tuvo conciencia de estar dando la misma
> réplica que recibió del coronel Aureliano Buendía en su
> celda de sentenciado, y una vez más se estremeció con la
> comprobación de que el tiempo no pasaba, como ella lo
> acaba de admitir, sino que daba vueltas en redondo
> (284-85).

There is no need to go into the fusion of present, past, and
future, as exemplified in the first sentence and in many other respects, in the narrative structure of *Cien años*. Critics have written extensively on the implications of this feature of the novel.
It should be stressed, however, that the novelist's penchant for
circular structures entails an internal pre-text. By anticipating at
the beginning of certain chapters the events which will follow,
the novelist creates a pre-text which then serves as a general out-
line on which he expands.

In *Crónica*, the past and the present converge in the characters' memories of the incidents surrounding the murder of
Santiago Nasar some twenty-seven years earlier. Assuming the
role of an investigative reporter, the narrator compares his task
of gathering information to trying to "recomponer con tantas
astillas dispersas el espejo roto de la memoria" (13). Among
other achievements, the novel is an exploration of the elusiveness of reality.[7] It also explores the role played by ideology, bias,
prejudice, self-aggrandizement, malice, human weakness, and
the passage of time in distorting the memory of past events. The
bewildering perspectives from which the murder of Santiago is
viewed and the diverse discourses they entail exemplify *par excellence* the novelist's "dialogic imagination."

The carnivalesque tradition, as Bakhtin affirms, con-
stantly undermines in manifold ways what is ready-made, the
"official version" of reality, and the established social order (273-
74). The official version of reality presents itself as the natural
order of society. The "carnivalized consciousness" incessantly
seeks to subvert that "natural" order.[8]

Like other novelists with a carnivalized consciousness,
García Márquez juxtaposes to the world presented by "official
culture" a novelistic world that relentlessly challenges and sub-

verts that world of established values. His magical realism in *Cien años* and other works provides him, along with other techniques, a framework within which to laugh at, mock, parody, exaggerate, and in general dramatize the follies of official culture, just as Cervantes challenged the official culture of his time within the framework of Don Quixote's madness (See Bakhtin on *Don Quixote's* grotesque realism, 22-23, 65, 103, 201, 434).

The novel's constant challenge of official culture is sharply focused, made explicit, in the presentation of events surrounding the banana strike. José Arcadio Segundo, having observed, before losing consciousness, the massacre of some three thousand banana strikers and their supporters, awakens in the night to find himself surrounded by corpses. Stacked like bunches of bananas in the boxcars of what appears to be an endless train, the bodies are enroute to the sea, into which they will be surreptitiously dumped. He escapes from the train, but discovers that everyone he meets denies that the massacre took place. The only survivor, he is determined that the truth will be kept alive. To this end he tells his brother Aureliano Segundo and the child Aureliano the true version of the event. Later, Aureliano scandalizes Fernanda by repeating this version (295-96). Before he dies, José Arcadio Segundo's last act is to urge Aureliano to remember what happened: "—Acuérdate siempre de que eran más de tres mil y que los echaron al mar" (300).

Despite José Arcadio Segundo's efforts, the official version of the outcome of the strike is ultimately accepted:

> La versión oficial, mil veces repetida y machacada en todo el país por cuanto medio de divulgación encontró el gobierno a su alcance, terminó por imponerse: no hubo muertos, los trabajadores satisfechos habían vuelto con sus familias, y la compañía bananera suspendía actividades mientras pasaba la lluvia (263).

At night, however, the government soldiers swept through the city arresting potential troublemakers:

> En la noche, después del toque de queda, derribaban puertas a culetazos, sacaban a los sospechosos de sus camas y se las llevaban a un viaje sin regreso. Era todavía la búsqueda y el exterminio de los malhechores, asesinos, incendiarios y revoltosos del Decreto Número cuatro, pero los militares lo negaban a los propios pari-

entes de sus víctimas, que desbordaban la oficina de los
comandantes en busca de noticias (263).

The official version eventually appears in school text-
books and legal transcripts. When Aureliano attempts to refute
this version, his listeners respond: ". . . [D]espués de todo había
quedado establecido en expendientes y en los textos de escuela
primaria: que la compañía bananera no había existido nunca"
(329).

This whole episode involves a reversal of categories. History, a nonfictional type of discourse, becomes fiction, while literature, a fictional type of discourse, tells the historical truth.
Words conceal as well as reveal. The novel blurs the distinction
between the two types of discourse, privileging literature over
history. As linguistic constructs, both history and literature are
on the same footing. *Cien años* reveals how the interpretation
of history is distorted by those in power, by those with the tools
for a more powerful discourse. History is interpretation. Yet, in
exposing the weakness of history or "official versions," literature
is its loyal opposition, pruning with its skepticism and correc-
tions the rotten branches of falsehood and distortion.

As critics have often noted, exaggeration is an essential
characteristic of García Márquez's style, especially in those works
in which magical realism is prominent, but also in works in
which other types of discourse play a prominent role. This hyperbolism probably has many origins, and certainly produces
manifold effects. One probable source is Faulkner; then there are
the mythological and biblical models, as well as those of chivalric romances. Yet another, as the novelist indicated in his Nobel
address, is the quest for an adequate means of presenting the
"outsized" and "unbridled reality" of Latin America. But, again,
such exaggeration is very Rabelaisian. Rabelaisian exaggeration
provides an excellent model for presenting the "unbridled reality" of Latin America. As Bakhtin affirms, folk festivals and carnival forms involved "a pronounced hyperbolism of bodily
images, especially those of eating and drinking. Exaggeration
characterized both grotesque realism and folk festival forms . . ."
(63). Writing of the exaggerated size of foodstuffs, Bakhtin
stresses the positive significance of size and quality in such
images:

> Indeed, one of the oldest forms of hyperbolic grotesque
> was the exaggerated size of foodstuffs. In this exagger-

ated form of valuable matter we see for the first time
the positive and absolute meaning of size and quantity
in an aesthetic image. Hyperboles of food parallel the
most ancient parallel of belly, mouth, and phallus
(184).

Examples of such exaggeration abound on almost every
page of *Cien años*. The insomnia plague, José Arcadio Buendía's
gigantic size, his astonishing feats of strength, his unbridled sen-
sual appetites, and his enormous phallus are obviously Rabelaisian hyperboles. The eating contest between Aureliano Segundo and Camila Sagastume, referred to above, is no less so.
The longevity of characters such as Ursula and Petra Cotes is
both biblical and Rabelaisian. The rainfall that lasts four years,
eleven months, and two days is yet another example of the novel's relentlessly hyperbolic style. There is no point in continuing
to enumerate the myriad examples of Rabelaisian hyperbole;
anyone who has read the novel can easily come up with dozens.
Less obvious, because magical realism is no longer present, is the
hyperbolism of *Crónica*. After all, ostensibly the style is that of
an investigative reporter, who presumably wishes to report in as
objective a fashion as possible what others report to him. This,
for the most part, he seems to do. The exaggeration derives from
the events themselves—the words and deeds of the characters.
The murder itself, one of the goriest and most vivid ever rendered in literature, the extreme mutilation of Santiago Nasar's
body during the autopsy, the extravagance of the wedding celebration, and the impotence of the townspeople to stop a murder
announced so often to so many are major examples of the exaggeration of carnivalized discourse.
     Perhaps not so obvious is the crowing of some two hun-
dred roosters gathered at the dock for the bishop's coxcomb soup.
When the bishop's boat toots its horn, the roosters begin to crow,
provoking the crowing of all the roosters in the town. The narrator exclaims: "Era un alboroto tan grande que no podía creerse
que hubiera tantos gallos en el pueblo, y pensé que venían en el
buque del obispo . . ." (22, 26, 27). This incident echoes the crowing of the cock when Peter betrayed Christ; the bishop betrays the
townspeople when he fails to disembark in the town. Another
case is the almost two thousand letters Angel Vicario writes to
Bayardo San Román, who returns them unopened to her in person. Sheer quantity becomes quality, revealing the intensity and
persistence of Angela's love and, ultimately, in his saving and

return in person of the letters, Bayardo's returning of her love. The inability of the Vicario twins and the narrator to rid themselves of the odor of Santiago's mutilated body (103, 104) are additional examples of carnivalesque exaggeration. So are the ailments the twins suffer in jail while awaiting trial: Pablo cannot stop urinating, twice causing the portable latrine to overflow, and Pedro cannot urinate at all (104, 105). Carnivalesque hyperbole, then, is not limited to the style of magical realism in García Márquez's fiction, but is a fundamental structural element that can pop up anywhere in his narrative fiction. Such exaggeration also contributes in a fundamental way to the symbolic implications of his fiction.

Laughter is a constant element of carnivalesque discourse. Presupposing freedom from fear, confusion, and dogmatism, laughter parodies, and thereby corrects, the one-sided seriousness of all that is official and petrified in ceremonial form and dogma. As Bakhtin says, carnivalesque laughter does not gainsay seriousness but complements it:

> True ambivalent and universal laughter does not deny
> seriousness but purifies and completes it. Laughter pu-
> rifies from dogmatism, from the intolerant and the pet-
> rified; it liberates from fanaticism and pedantry, from
> fear and intimidation, from didacticism, naïveté and
> illusion, from the single meaning, the single level, from
> sentimentality. Laughter does not permit seriousness to
> atrophy and to be torn away from the one being, forever
> incomplete. It restores this ambivalent wholeness (122-
> 23).

Anyone who has read *Cien años* even in the most cursory fashion knows that, though it is a serious book, the comic is one of its dominant elements, and as indicated above, the most frequent comic mode is hyperbole. Its pages are suffused with language that elicits the reader's laughter. Since the ubiquity of humor in the novel precludes an exhaustive analysis here, perhaps a better procedure is to attempt to illuminate the distinctive carnivalesque flavor of the novel's humor by comparing and contrasting the treatment of a single theme with that of another outstanding Hispanic writer: García Lorca. Since puritanism is an important theme both in *Cien años* and Lorca's *La casa de Bernard Alba*, a brief comparison should be revealing. Both works militate against a narrow, Catholic morality centered largely around the aversion to bodily functions and, especially, to human sexuality. This the main thrust of *Bernarda Alba*, and notwithstanding its prominence in *Cien años*, it is but one of many facets of the novel. As corresponds to a play, the dramatic tension in *Bernarda Alba*, is constant and builds as the play progresses. The dramatic tension is reinforced by an oppressive (and symbolic) nature. So fanatical is Bernarda in her will to impose her puritanical values on her daughters that the resultant tone of the play is bitingly satirical. There is a kind of grim humor in the exaggeration of her personality and especially in her tremendous self-deception, but this remains below the surface. She is more a character to be feared and hated than to be laughed at. Although her actions may be tinged with hysteria when she shouts at the end of the play, "Mi hija ha muerto virgen" (123), notwithstanding the strong smell of irony, the tone is serious rather than mocking. Despite all that has happened, Bernarda continues to attempt to impose her will on reality and to maintain appearances; and no other character in the play is strong enough to challenge her. The reader feels outrage at her inability to learn from her own experience and at her insistence on having her way whatever the cost. Bernarda's monstrosity is raised to a new level with her final act, and she is not a funny monster.

In *Cien años*, on the other hand, Amaranta's theatrical death is presented within a framework of gaiety and celebration. Just beneath her matter-of-fact tone in which the narrator describes her insistence that Ursula certify that she is dying a virgin lies a mocking tone. Consider also Fernanda's prudish language (183, 268), referred to above, and her correspondence with "the invisible doctors," in order to avoid exposing her body to a local doctor (269-70).

The differences between the two approaches can perhaps be best illustrated by a comparison between two similar incidents in the two works. In a well-known incident in *Bernarda Alba*, a stallion kicks hard against a stable wall adjacent to Bernarda's house. Bernarda explains to a Prudencia, a visitor in her home at that moment that the noise was made by her stallion; he senses the nearby presence of the mares. Bernarda explains that the mares are in heat and will be bred the following day. Prudencia remarks that Bernarda has been very successful in increasing her livestock (93-94). Ironically, this same sexual force is present in Bernarda's daughters, but she is blinded by the delusion that she can control nature itself.

In a similar incident in *Cien años*, one night when Aureliano Segundo is with Petra Cotes, he hears loud noises on the patio wall:

> Pero una noche cuando ya nadie en el pueblo quería oir hablar de las rifas de conejos, sintió un estruendo en la pared de patio. "No te asustes," dijo Petra Cotes. "Son los conejos." No pudieron dormir más, atormentados por el tráfago de los animales. Al amanecer, Aureliano segundo abrió la puerta y vio el patio empedrado de conejos, azules en el resplandor del alba (167).

Observing the rapid multiplication of the rabbits, Aureliano Segundo suggests that Petra switch to cows. She follows this advice, and the herd also begins to multiply. García Márquez borrows this episode from Lorca's play, but presents it within the framework of gaiety and hyperbolic humor. The Colombian writer, like his Spanish model, explores the polar opposition of sterility/fertility with a serious intention, but, unlike Lorca, treats the matter humorously as befits carnivalized discourse.

Notes

[1] In *Historia de un deicidio* Vargas Llosa writes at some length on what he calls García Márquez's "demonios culturales," including Rabelais as a significant "demonio" (169-76); Mallet finds Rabelaisian elements in "los funerales de la Mamá Grande"; Sims persuasively demonstrates how García Márquez creates an "espacio carnavelesco" as one of several "macroelementos" fundamental to the structure of his fiction: *passim*; Palencia-Roth makes a compelling case for the presence of certain intertexts in *El otoño del patriarca*, specifically the presence in the novel of Plutarch's and Suetonius's lives of Julius Caesar, *El diario* of Columbus, and Rubén Darío; Bell-Villada gives a general account of Rabelais's influence on García Márquez's work. As I was completing this study, I became aware of Rodríguez-Vergara's study of satire in García Márquez's work. Her book deals with the satirical elements in the novelist's four most recent novels within the framework of the ideas of Bakhtin, Highet, and Menippean satire. In *Crónica*, the only work we study in common from a Bakhtinian perspective, she analyzes the parodic elements.

[2] What García Márquez does in Latin America is not unlike Galdós's attempt in the nineteenth century to bring a belated secular Reformation to Spain. Both writers' works challenge the absolutisms of a persistent and all too pervasive medievalism in Hispanic culture.

[3] Randolph D. Pope has suggested that García Márquez's distrust of theory issues from the novelist's anti-intellectualism (196). This seems quite feasible, but I suspect that García Márquez has something of the pragmatist's

reservations about the uses of theory. It is hard to argue with Carmen Arnau's succint judgment: "Los personajes de *Cien años de soledad* no piensan mucho, se dejan simplemente llevar por sus deseos, por sus instintos . . ." (121). In his study of *Cien años*, Michael Woods finds no useful historical perspective structured into the novel: "The [characters'] readings are usually ignorant or deluded, and often trying to get rid of history entirely. But García Márquez presents no rival or superior reading. The shape of his novel is the shape of the superstitions it contains—this is why the novel can seem hopeless—and the writer displays only skepticism, patience and will; and a refusal of hypocrisy and all pretensions to wisdom. But this is a considerable display, however quiet-seeming, and in itself a liberation because it allows us both to know and to disbelieve the most enchanting and seemingly indispensable of myths" (11). Although this is largely true, in my judgment it is overstated. After all, the word *soledad* in the title and the many examples of the various types of solitude exemplified in the novel imply a specific perspective on the novelist's part. Discovering the content of this perspective requires a strong collaborative effort on the reader's part. How does solitude manifest itself in each of the characters? What are the opposites of solitude? In an interview somewhere, the novelist has noted the inability of the Buendías to love and their lack of solidarity with others.

4 For a more detailed discussion of the theme of the primacy of the body in *Crónica*, see Arnold M. Penuel, "The Sleep of Vital Reason in García Márquez's *Crónica de una muerte anunciada*."

5 See Arnold M. Penuel, "Death and the Maiden: The Demythologization of Virginity in *Cien años de soledad*," for a study of Amaranta.

6 For example, Graciela Maturo, *Claves simbólicas de García Márquez*.

7 In this respect García Márquez does what Galdós did about a hundred years earlier in his companion novels *La incógnita* and *Realidad*. Galdós's novels were also inspired by a well-known crime, though the crime itself is not the subject of the novels but rather the nature and elusiveness of reality.

8 Bakhtin's view of "official culture" resembles Roland Barthes view of the "naturalization" of language itself. Language is presented as "natural" by individuals or groups seeking power through a particular type of discourse. See Terry Eagleton: 136.

Chapter 5

The Theme of Colonialism in
"La increíble y triste historia de la cándida Eréndira
y de su abuela desalmada"

Such is the transformative power of García Márquez's literary imagination, so numerous and ambiguous are the allusive elements present in a given work, that the reader is nearly always forced into a strenuous effort of collaboration with the author to detect even the most tenuous patterns of meaning. The Colombian writer submits his intertexts to a dicing and chopping process that leaves them well disguised in his final recipe. The allusions that abound throughout his works entice the reader to seek deeper patterns of meaning, but rarely yield their meanings in an exclusively straightforward manner. García Márquez employs a combination of straightforwardness, obliqueness, displacement of referent and object, and a host of other techniques to keep the reader off balance and distanced from the work's deeper levels of meaning.

Typical in this respect is his novella-length story, "La increíble y triste historia de la cándida Eréndira y de su abuela desalmada," which in the decade and a half since its appearance has been extraordinarily stubborn about yielding recondite meanings to its readers. This probably explains the relative paucity of criticism on the story. Yet "Eréndira" is replete with tantalizing allusive elements, suggestive of further interpretive horizons to be explored. The conclusion I have reached, after many readings, is that "Eréndira" is ultimately a complex literary statement, similar to a parable, on the nature of the relations between Spain and its American colonies and, by extension, on the nature of colonialism itself. While no detail viewed in isolation

decisively cinches this interpretation, in my judgment a combination of details, allusions, and parallels constitutes compelling
evidence for such a reading of the story.

In "Eréndira" García Márquez reinterprets the process of
colonization and its animating ethos through a symbolic portrayal of Spain's colonization of America. He had already manifested his hostility to both colonial and imperial exploitation in
Cien años, especially in the exploitation by the foreign banana
company and, later, in *El otoño del patriarca* (1975), whose titular
protagonist is largely a creation of a foreign power. Michael
Palencia-Roth certainly hits the mark in writing of García
Márquez's "profound anticolonialism" (22-23). Although their
approach is quite different from mine, Antonio Benítez Rojo
and Hilda O. Benítez in an interesting and ingenious interpretation reach a similar conclusion with respect to the theme of
colonialism in "Eréndira":

> Así las cosas, hay que concluir que el texto de García
> Márquez intenta entronizarse en lugar del significante
> fálico, tanto en lo que atañe el viejo mito patriarcal
> como en lo que atañe al orden despótico, corrupto y de-
> pendiente que dejó en América Latina la colonización
> europea. El mito de Eréndira se nos presenta entonces
> como una alternativa que atenta de lleno contra occi-
> dente en lo que éste haya significado un modelo repre-
> sivo para América Latina (1075).

But what evidence do we find in "Eréndira" that the story
is an attack on colonialism? The most obvious evidence is the
relations between the grandmother and Eréndira, in which the
granddaughter finally rebels against the older woman's exploitation and, with the help of her lover, Ulises, obtains her freedom.
The grandmother's total ascendancy over her illegitimate
granddaughter is matched by the total submission of the latter.
The respective psychologies of the two characters complement
each other, fitting like hand in glove, just as colonial relations
require a colonial power disposed to command, and colonies
disposed to obey. Of the implications in the story for colonial
mentality, I shall say more later.

From the outset the grandmother evokes a Spain which,
though decadent, still holds sway over its colonies. The fact that
she is referred to throughout the story only as *abuela* underscores her status as a role-player and abstraction or archetype

rather than as an individual. Her enormous body, "como una muñeca más grande que el tamaño humano" (98) suggests the sheer size and dominating physical presence of the Spanish empire. The description of "los cabellos metálicos y sueltos, en el hombro potente tatuado sin piedad con un escarnio de marineros" (97) refers to the grandmother's past life as a prostitute and evokes the marks left on the Iberian peninsula by the sailors, traders, and invaders who through the centuries exploited its wealth.

The grandmother's nostalgia for the past, manifested in her dreams and memories, her prepossessing presence in which "se notaba el dominio de una grandeza anticuada" (98), her "sueños de grandeza" (99), and especially her veneration of the memory and tombs of the two Amadises, all associate her with a Spain that has seen better times. Particularly significant is her worship of the memory of the Amadises. Although of unknown national origin, *Amadís de Gaula* gave rise to the chivalric novel in Spain, whose cycle ended with the appearance of Cervantes's *Don Quixote*. As Angel Rosenblatt has noted, "*El Amadís* llegó a ser el código caballeresco en la vida española y francesa en gran parte del siglo XVI" (8). Remarking on the value of this genre's popularity in Spain in revealing national character, Rosenblatt adds: "La novela de caballerías se convirtió, gracias a Amadis y su estirpe en expresión del genio nacional" (10). It is a commonplace among historians, of course, that the Iberian conquerors of the New World were imbued with the spirit of the chivalric novels, though they, like Don Quixote, found ways to subordinate these ideals to their own ambitions and desires. In an extended conversation with Miguel Fernández-Braso, García Márquez himself asserts that "a nuestros abuelos les dejaron embriagados de literatura de caballerías" (94). The first description of García Márquez's Amadís makes it clear that he, like his literary forebear, also acquired fame:[1]

> Aquel refugio incomprensible había sido construido por el marido de la abuela, un contrabandista legendario, que se llamaba Amadis, con quien ella tuvo un hijo que, también se llamaba Amadis, y que fue el padre de Eréndira (99).

Just as the origin of *Amadís de Gaula* is unknown, in "Eréndira" "nadie conoció los origenes ni los motivos de esa familia" (99).

And, again, just as the original chivalric novel gave rise to numerous offspring, "Eréndira"'s Amadís has a son, also named Amadís, and numerous emulators in his profession as a smuggler, whose aid the grandmother seeks to rescue Eréndira from the missionaries:

> Parecía una réplica de los Amadises, con una garra de
> ala volteada, botas altas, dos cananas cruzadas en el
> pecho, un fusil militar y dos pistolas (124).

Note also that these Amadises wear the modern equivalents of their ancient forebears' "uniform" and armor.

Further details also point to a strong association with *Amadís de Gaula* and, by extension, with chivalric ideals. To lend authority to her plea to the smuggler for aid, the grandmother dramatically announces: "Soy la Dama" (125), playing the role of the lady in distress of knight errantry. The allusion to her former beauty in superlative terms, even in this situation, reinforces the episode's chivalric framework:

> [The smuggler] contempló un instante el rostro estragado
> por la vigilia, los ojos apagados de cansancio, el cabello
> marchito de la mujer que aún a su edad, en su mal estado
> y con aquella luz cruda en la cara hubiera podido decir
> que había sido la más bella del mundo (125).[2]

Moreover, the mobility of the smugglers and the sailors, who have admired and enjoyed the grandmother's beauty, parallels the adventurous errantry of their chivalric predecessors.

Still, in keeping with García Márquez's ironic intent, it is evident that the Amadises, as well as the grandmother, epitomize more the self-serving conduct dramatized in *Lazarillo de Tormes* and *La Celestina* than the traits idealized in *Amadís de Gaula*. It is partly a question of appearances versus reality. Although the parallels are less pointed than in the case of the chivalric tradition, the echoes of *La Celestina* in "Eréndira" are too insistent to be passed over. The grandmother's age, her status as a former prostitute turned procuress, her greed, her energy and domination of all about her, her obvious joy in her profession, and the miscalculations that result in her murder, identify her with the great Spanish bawd. Sempronio and Pármeno are combined in the portrayal of the photographer, who profits from the grandmother's business, and who, like his literary predecessors, is undone by his own greed. Angered by his refusal to share the costs of paying the musicians who play for Eréndira's customers, the grandmother is later instrumental in his death, when she tells the authorities that he is the accomplice of the fleeing Eréndira and Ulises.

The grandmother's location in the desert symbolizes Spain's physical and cultural isolation from the rest of Europe as well as the arid, spiritual sterility of her relations with her American colonies.

Although the setting is more or less contemporary, and while no single relationship or detail is decisive, as indicated above, the cumulative evidence that the story parabolically defines the nature of Spain's relations with her American colonies is ubiquitous. This symbolism is reinforced through the grandmother's association with *Amadís de Gaula* and *La Celestina*, through other particulars of her relations with Eréndira, her illegitimate granddaughter, through her associations with others, and through the Indians who serve her. The most obvious parallel, of course, is her unconscionable exploitation of Eréndira. Eréndira's illegitimacy serves as a vague pretext for this exploitation. Her status as the younger Amadis' bastard daughter resembles the inferior status of the Indians as well as that of the colonists *vis-à-vis* the mother country, a fundamental condition of their exploitation. In a characteristic displacement Eréndira's name itself suggests her primary function, and that of the colonies. By dropping the initial "E" and shifting the accent mark to the "a" it becomes "rendirá" with the optional meanings "she will yield," "she will render," or, if used reflexively, even "she will surrender." From the grandmother's perspective these are her principal functions. George R. McMurray has focused on the transitive meaning "to conquer," which he believes to be appropriate in view of her final triumph over the other characters (113). In my view, for reasons that will be made clear below, Eréndira's triumph leaves much to be desired, a fact that McMurray recognizes when he writes of the "pessimistic assessment of the human endeavor" implicit in the story's conclusion (112). By symbolic extension, the story suggests that whatever idealistic reasons Spaniards, and historians may have advanced for Spain's conquest and colonization of the New World, the most important animating force and the one that shaped the country's relations with its colonies was the profit motive. The colonial relations provided an opportunity for maximum exploitation with minimal economic, legal, and moral constraints. Though decadent, during most of the colonial period, Spain, like the grandmother in her relations with Eréndira, was able to maintain an illusion of grandeur through the wealth extracted from its colonies.

What other relations and events in "Eréndira" evoke a colonial situation? Besides the grandmother's prepossessing physical presence, she exercises absolute authority over Eréndira; and she is able to dominate events and all those around her to get her way. When Ulises suggests to Eréndira that they flee together, she replies: "Nadie puede irse para ninguna parte sin permiso de su abuela" (136). Moreover, the unceasing tasks which the grandmother orders Eréndira to perform (98-102) parallel the endless tasks the mother country requires of its colonies. Early in the story, even the description of the grandmother's cistern suggests the Spanish exploitation of the Indians, and anticipates Spain's dependence on Indian labor and devious means of lowering their pay (140): "Tenía en el patio una cisterna para almacenar durante muchos años el agua llevada a lomo de indio desde manantiales remotos" (98). Originally, of course, the gold the grandmother accumulates was carried out of mines on Indian backs. She keeps the bars of gold she accumulates through Eréndira's prostitution in a vest worn beneath her blouse. The material of which the vest is made recalls Spain's mode of transporting gold to the peninsula in colonial times. The increase in the grandmother's size and the comparison of the ingots with bullets in a cartridge belt further remind the reader that the expansion of the Spanish empire was financed by gold and achieved by force of arms.

> Su tamaño monumental había aumentado, porque
> usaba debajo de la blusa un chaleco de lona de velero, en
> el cual se metía los lingotes de oro como se meten las
> balas en un cinturón de cartucheras (148).[3]

It is literally gold, a gold chain, that ties Eréndira to her bed, earning profits for the grandmother (147). Because of its value and great importance to Spaniards during the colonial period, gold serves as a synechdoche for the manifold riches Spain reaped from the colonies. Despite its decline beginning in the latter part of the 17th century, thanks to the wealth of its colonies, Spain was still able to keep itself afloat economically, and was able to continue nourishing illusions of grandeur. Because of Eréndira's sacrifices the grandmother is able not only to keep herself afloat, but also to surround herself with considerable luxury, albeit her dwelling place has degenerated from a mansion to a used circus tent. She continues, however, to nourish dreams of grandeur:

> Cuando los Amadíses murieron el uno de fiebres melancólicas, y el otro acribillado en un pleito de rivales, la mujer enterró los cadáverers en el patio, despachó a las catorce sirvientas descalzas, y siguió apacentando sus sueños de grandeza en la penumbra de la casa furtiva, gracias al sacrificio de la nieta bastarda que había criado desde el nacimiento (99).

"Eréndira" also illuminates Spain's relations with its colonies through the evocation of a colonial atmosphere of improvisation, diversity, and virtual lawlessness. The grandmother's mode of living, her nomadic tent life, epitomizes the principle of improvisation. The smugglers' way of earning their livelihood also contributes to the atmosphere of improvisation and exemplifies the lawlessness of the region. Smuggling seems to be the chief means of earning a living in the desert. The smugglers are brazen and well armed, sometimes plying their trade in broad daylight in open defiance—or perhaps with the collusion—of the authorities (141-42). As for the diversity of activities and people in the desert, the atmosphere is carnivalesque. The variety is evident in the description of the line of men waiting to pay for a moment of pleasure with Eréndira:

> La fila interminable y ondulante, compuesta por hombres de razas y condiciones diversas, parecía una serpiente de vértebras humanas que dormitaba a través de salones y plazas, por entre bazares abigarrados y mercados ruidosos, y se salía de las calles de aquella ciudad fragorosa de traficantes de paso. Cada calle era un garito público, cada casa una cantina, cada puerta un refugio de prófugos. Las numerosas músicas indescifrables y los pregones gritados formaban un solo estruendo de pánico en el calor alucinante (146).[4]

The narrator goes on to speak of "la muchedumbre de apátridas" and "mujeres venidas de los cuatro cuadrantes de la rosa náutica" (146).

The almost rhythmical appearance of certain motifs suggestive of colonial, imperial, and episcopal power reinforces the theme of colonial exploitation. From the charred ruins of her mansion the grandmother salvages a "cama virreinal" and a "trono chamuscado" (106). Shortly afterwards, we learn that the throne has been restored (111), and later, we read that "la cama de la abuela había recuperado su esplendor virreinal" (135). The grandmother presides over all her affairs seated on the throne. The first time she moved with Eréndira to another town "la abuela esperó sentada en el trono, en medio de la calle, hasta que acabaron de bajar de carga" (107, see also 111, 124, 155). Thanks to Eréndira's sacrifice, the grandmother travels in imperial splendor on a palanquin shaded by an ecclesiastical canopy:

> Nunca se vio tanta opulencia junta por aquellos *reinos* de pobres. Era un desfile de carretas tirados por bueyes, sobre las cuales se amontonaban algunas réplicas de pacotilla de la parafernalia extinguida con el desastre de la mansión, y no sólo los *bustos imperiales* y los relojes raros, sino también un piano de ocasión y una vitrola de maniqueta con los discos de la nostalgia. Una recua de indios se ocupaba de la carga, y una banda de músicos anunciaba en los pueblos su *llegada triunfal* (148, emphasis added).

This passage clothes the grandmother's activities and mode of living in imperial images and also makes clear the gross disparities between her life style and that of her "subjects."

The reference to the "palio de iglesia" is one of several oblique references to the supportive role, however ambiguous at times, the Church played in the conquest and colonization of the New World. The ecclesiastical canopy protects the grandmother against the burning equatorial sun just as her "báculo que parecía de obispo" (98) supports her enormous weight when she must get about on foot. The "báculo" is mentioned twice in the same sentence with the word "trono":

> Apoyada en el báculo episcopal, la abuela abandonó el tenderete y se sentó en el trono a esperar el paso de las mulas (109).

> La abuela se incorporó en el trono blandiendo el báculo amenazador cuando lo [Ulises] vio entrar en la carpa con el pastel de fiesta (155).

On another occasion, it is referred to as the "báculo devastador," and on the same page we read that the grandmother remained "en guardia con el báculo" (115). By symbolic extension, the grandmother's walking stick dramatizes how the Crown used the Church both as a source of support and a weapon in its colonial enterprises.

How does this square with the grandmother's conflict with the representatives of the Church? First, one must note the peninsular origin of the missionaries. When the grandmother hears their peninsular diction, she deems necessary an indirect approach to avoid provoking them into a characteristic uncompromising stance (121-22). From the outset, the dispute is jurisdictional; one of the missionaries warns the grandmother and her retinue not to cross a line formed by a crack in the desert floor. When she replies that the desert belongs to no one, her antagonist responds: "Es de Dios . . ., y estáis violando sus santas leyes con vuestro tráfico inmundo" (121). The missionary then orders the grandmother to intern Eréndira in their convent. When she refuses, the missionaries stealthily remove her to the convent during the night. It seems clear from this incident that not only does the desert belong to God but also that his ministers aspire to exercise jurisdiction over those who inhabit it!

Despite the arduousness of her work in the convent, Eréndira considers herself happy there. This is a relative happiness, however; the Church's exploitation of her is simply much less rigorous than her secular exploitation:

> Era un oficio de mula, porque había un subir y bajar
> incesante de misioneros embarrados y novicios de carga,
> pero Eréndira lo sintió como un domingo de todos los
> días después de la galera mortal de la cama (126).

In the name of morality the missionaries force the pregnant young Indian women to marry their lovers, worsening the young women's situation, since the new husbands consider themselves justified in demanding more work of their spouses. While presented in a humorous fashion, this episode illustrates the ambiguous consequences of the Church's attempts to improve the lot of the Indian during the colonial period.

The conflict between the grandmother and the missionaries evokes the frequent conflicts between the colonists and the Church. Representatives of the Church, of whom Bartolomé de las Casas is the best known, attacked their compatriots' abusive treatment of the Indians and the exploitation of their labor. The Church's will to protect the Indians is revealed here to be frus-

trated by a narrow-minded and unintelligent morality, encom-
passing its own form of exploitation.

   If the Church is far too narrow in its conception of morality, civil authority is excessively generous, especially with regard
to the exploitation of the weak. Despite her reprehensible abuse
of Eréndira, the grandmother is able to obtain a letter from senator Onésimo Sánchez vouching for her good conduct: ". . . [P]ues
la abuela había conseguido que el senador avalara su moralidad
con una carta de su puño y letra, y se iba abriendo con ella las
puertas mejor trancadas del desierto" (134). This Senator's letter
enables her to enlist the unhesitating aid of the illiterate com-
mander of the local military corps to pursue the fleeing Eréndira
and Ulises (141), leading to their capture and the death of the
photographer. This episode underscores the collaborative roles
played by the civil and military authorities in the colonial period
to aid the wealthy and powerful in their exploitative enterprises.
Without explicitly discussing the theme of colonialism, Raymond Williams has clearly observed the pattern of exploitation
in "Eréndira":

> The paradigm of exploitation is clearly delineated
> with the grandmother, the military, and the govern-
> ment representing the exploiters. In addition to the di-
> rect collaboration the grandmother receives from the
> military and a senator, it is notable that the primary
> users of Eréndira's sexual services are soldiers (104-05).

   As in the colonial period, civil and military authorities
are scarcely distinguishable: the grandmother "recurrió a la autoridad civil, que era ejercida por un militar" (122). In her first
encounter with this official, who serves as mayor of the town,
she finds him occupied in a futile effort to produce rainfall by
shooting holes through a cloud. Is this an oblique commentary
on the ultimate sterility of colonial civil-military activities, on
the fundamental incapacity of the authorities for producing anything of real benefit to the masses of colonial subjects they gov-
erned? García Márquez has shown us a senator who is illiterate
and a mayor who tries to make rain by shooting at a cloud. In
my judgment, these situations are designed to create a perception of the corruption, incompetence, and sterility that are the
warp and woof of the colonial enterprise.

   With respect to the military presence, soldiers compose a
large proportion of Eréndira's customers. Their ubiquitous pres-

ence corresponds to their omnipresence in the colonization of
Spanish America and, indirectly, to the role that raw force played
in the process.

Eréndira's passage from a state of total submission to her
grandmother to an intense desire for freedom leading to the
conspiracy with Ulises to kill the grandmother parallels the
colonies' struggle for independence. Ulises' ineffectual attempts
to end the grandmother's life with rat poison and explosives
suggest the premature efforts of numerous figures like Father
Miguel de Hidalgo of Mexico to achieve independence. It should
be noted in passing, however, that the grandmother's loss of her
hair after eating the rat poison presages her demise; her loss of
hair symbolically prefigures her loss of strength.

The awakening to and quest for freedom is a central part
of the story which is developed through the actions of both
Eréndira and Ulises. Eréndira's mode of being indicates a
scarcely formed identity and that she has assimilated the grandmother's expectations of her as her logical and proper role in
life. This is the physical significance of the sonambulistic state in
which she performs her tasks: "Cerró los ojos, los abrió después
con una expresión sin cansancio, y empezó a echar la sopa en la
sopera. Trabajaba dormida (100).[5] Such is her submissiveness
that she utters not the slightest complaint when the grandmother calculates her enormous debt and the interminable years
of prostitution that will be required to pay it (103, 112). Also in-
dicative of Eréndira's fearful assimilation of the role her grandmother forces on her is the instinctive fear with which she interrupts the infatuated loader when he tells the grandmother he
would like to take Eréndira with him:

> La niña intervino asustada.
> —Yo no he dicho nada (108).

The assimilation of this role is further demonstrated when
Eréndira is given the choice to live with her new Indian husband or return to her grandmother; she chooses, without hesita-
tion, to return. Eréndira's choice corresponds to the colonies assimilation of Spanish or European culture in the development
of their dominant identity. Eréndira's somnambulism and the
details of her internalization of the role the grandmother pre-
pares for her before she is old enough and strong enough to
protest parallel the colonies assimilation of the stronger, more

prestigious European culture before they are strong enough and sufficiently aware of the possibilities of developing their own cultural patterns. By the time they do achieve independence the Spanish ethos—and language—has become an indelible part of the identity of the new ruling classes.

The colonies' enchantment with Spain is based on a combination of fear and admiration of a stronger, superior civilization, along with the hope for greater material prosperity their colonial relations seem to promise. Eréndira's bewitchment by her grandmother is evident in her decision to return to the old woman: "Eréndira se encontró de nuevo bajo el hechizo que la había dominado desde su nacimiento" (130). Later, when she hears the signal she and Ulises had agreed upon for their flight, she is finally able to summon the energy to escape her grandmother's magnetic pull: "Se asomó a la noche hasta que volvió a cantar la lechuza, y su instinto de libertad prevaleció por fin contra el hechizo de la abuela" (140).

By the time the grandmother begins to hold up the enticement of luxury and prestige to Eréndira, the latter's yearning for freedom is too strong and makes her oblivious to the old woman's words:

> —Serás una dueña—le dijo—. Una dama de alcurnia venerada por tus protegidas, y complacida y honrada por las más altas autoridades. Los capitanes de los buques te mandarán postales desde todos los puertos del mundo. Eréndira no la escuchaba (149-50).

The narrator prefaces the grandmother's predictions with the statement that a "a veces confundía sus nostalgias con la clarividencia del porvenir" (149). In the context of the total relations between Eréndira and her grandmother, this statement reveals the grandmother's efforts to impose her own past on her granddaughter's future and, symbolically, Spain's will to impose its outworn cultural patterns on its American colonies.

Ulises, with his "cara de ángel" (116, 155) brings Eréndira the message of freedom. The love between Ulises and Eréndira exercises a transformative influence on both young people. Both awaken to a strong desire for independence. Eréndira "se había vuelto espontánea y locuaz, como si la inocencia de Ulises le hubiera cambiado no sólo el humor, sino también la índole" (119). Ulises' love of Eréndira gives him the strength to break with his father and leave home in search of his beloved (151). This same love leads him to kill the grandmother. That the grandmother has been the main obstacle to Eréndira's achievement of an authentic identity as well as physical freedom is made dramatically clear in the young woman's reaction to her grandmother's death:

> Eréndira puso entonces el platón en una mesa, se inclinó sobre la abuela, escudriñándola sin tocarla, y cuando se convenció de que estaba muerta su rostro adquirió de golpe toda la madurez de persona mayor que no le habían dado sus veinte años de infortunio (162).[6]

The wind is an important *motif* in "Eréndira" that almost possesses the force of another character. It appears in both the initial and final sentences of the story.[7] The wind is a dynamic force associated with various characters' destinies and a destiny that determines the course of events in general. The wind represents fate in the form of external and internal forces conditioning the characters' conduct. Eréndira's "viento de la desgracia" (97), which turns over the candelabra against the curtains demonstrates the role of happenstance in the destinies of individuals and nations, how an accident can determine the sequence of events in a person or nation's life. Eréndira is forced into a life of prostitution through an accident. Columbus' discovery of the New World, if not altogether an accident, was a form of serendipity, since he was really seeking a new passage to Asia.

The wind is identified with the photographer's individual destiny, which is partly the result of initiative she and the grandmother take. When the grandmother inquires of his destination on one occasion, he replies: "Para donde me lleve el viento" (124). Significantly, it is the wind which prevents him from hearing the agent's order to halt just before he is shot. Of course, destiny here is also the resultant of the grandmother's resentment, which caused her to identify him as an accomplice in Eréndira and Ulises' flight.

In other contexts, the wind is associated symbolically with the peninsular cultural tradition represented by the grandmother and the missionaries. The wind blows violently when the missionaries confront the grandmother:

> Un grupo de misioneros con los crucifijos en alto se habían plantado hombro contra hombro en medio del

desierto. Un viento tan bravo como el de la desgracia
sacudía sus hábitos de cañamazo y sus barbas cerriles, y
apenas les permitía tenerse en pie (121).

Again, the wind is blowing fiercely when Eréndira must choose
whether to flee with Ulises or remain with her grandmother:
"Eréndira no le [the grandmother] puso atención, pues la
lechuza, la solicitaba con apremio tenaz en las pausas del viento,
y estaba atormentada por la incertidumbre" (140). Here, the
wind is associated with everything the grandmother represents
in her relations with Eréndira, especially the ready-made role
she has imposed on her granddaughter. Hence, she hears Ulises'
signals during the wind's pauses. Another path opens in her
life, beckoning to another destiny, one that promises eventual
freedom, but that can only be achieved through arduous struggle
against old habits. For this reason, Eréndira and Ulises must
drive against the wind in their attempt to escape. For the same
reason, after her grandmother's death Eréndira disappears into
the desert "corriendo contra el viento, más veloz que un ve-
nado" (162). The wind represents the Iberian cultural tradition
which is an external force to be reckoned with. At the same
time, Eréndira and, by symbolic extension, the colonies have in-
ternalized this tradition, however ambivalently, making true
freedom extremely difficult to attain, even after the tyrant's
death.

García Márquez's recourse to Greek mythology in
"Eréndira" is characteristically indirect, well-disguised, and a
well-integrated part of the work's meanings. Michael Palencia-
Roth perceptively associates Eréndira with Ariadne because of
Ulises' private name for her: Aridnere (155).[8] He is certainly on
target also in perceiving a demythifying intention in the evocation of the myth (156), although he does not associate the demythification with the theme of Spanish colonialism.

According to the Greek myth, Minos, the tyrannical King
of Crete, required his subjects the Athenians to render periodical
tribute by sending seven young men to be placed in a labyrinth
to be slain, and perhaps devoured, by the Minotaur, a creature
with the head of a bull and the body of a man. When Theseus,
the son of the King of Athens, came to Crete with the intention
of slaying the Minotaur, Minos' daughter Ariadne fell in love
with him and gave him a thread with which to find his way out
of the labyrinth. After slaying the monster and escaping from
the labyrinth, Theseus left Crete, taking Ariadne with him. But

for reasons that are not clear, he abandoned her on the island of Naxos.

Although García Márquez's re-creation of the myth involves name displacement, some role reversal, and elements of his own invention, his core material centers on the Theseus-Ariadne myth and the mythological figures directly and indirectly associated with this myth. For the most part, Ulises plays the role of Theseus. While his name provides a key to his mythological status in "Eréndira," it also serves, at least initially, to throw the reader off the track as to his functional mythological identity. Ulises' first encounter with the grandmother both points to his mythological status and explains why Eréndira-Ariadne falls in love with him: "Tenía un aura *irreal* y parecía visible en la penumbra por el fulgor propio de *belleza*" (116, emphasis added). One aspect of the role reversal is that Ulises must rescue Eréndira from the monster in the maze, from her grandmother. After the rescue, it is Eréndira-Ariadne who abandons Ulises-Theseus instead of the reverse as occurs in the original myth. In another role reversal, Ulises-Theseus attempts to liberate Eréndira-Ariadne with a fuse (the mythical thread) leading into the grandmother's tent to explosives placed under her piano. The episode in which Ulises-Theseus tries to kill the grandmother with rat poison may very well have been suggested by the incident in which Aegeus, the king of Athens, unaware that Theseus was his son, attempted to kill him with poisoned wine. When Aegeus suddenly recognized his son, he dashed his cup to the ground thus averting a tragedy. The grandmother of course simply fails to be affected by the rat poison, except for the loss of her hair.

Although Daedalus was not directly involved in the Theseus-Ariadne myth, it was he who constructed the labyrinth for Minos in which the Minotaur was imprisoned and from which he and his son Icarus fashioned wings of feathers and wax to escape after the king imprisoned them there.

Given García Márquez' penchant for displacement, it is probable that the references to Ulises' "cara de ángel" and his answer to the grandmother's admiring query about where he had left his wings are oblique allusions to the mythological world of Daedalus: "El que las tenía era mi abuelo—contestó con naturalidad—, pero nadie lo cree" (116). After all, Daedalus used his wings to obtain his freedom from Minos' labyrinth, and Ulises seeks his and Eréndira's freedom. A subsequent event suggesting a further connection of Ulises with the Daedalus-Icarus story is the relatively pointed coincidence between the gradual loss of the birds' feathers in the truck in which Eréndira and Ulises are fleeing as their pursuers overtake them. The birds exhibit a totally deplumed condition when the lovers are captured, paralleling Icarus' loss of his feathers when he flew too near the sun. Initially, the feathers assure the pursuers that they are on the right track: "Antes del mediodía empezaron a ver las plumas. Pasaban en el viento, y eran plumas de pájaros nuevos, y el holandés los conoció porque eran las de sus pájaros desplumados por el viento" (143). Later, Eréndira and Ulises seem to be included among the featherless birds captured in the truck: "La patrulla militar se la adelantó a la destartalada camioneta cargada de pájaros desplumados por el viento, hizo una curva forzada, y le cerró el camino" (143).[9] The wind literally strips the birds of their feathers and symbolically strips Eréndira and Ulises of their freedom. "Eréndira" evinces yet another connection with Daedalus. An ingenious engineer, Daedalus designed a bath fitted with pipes through which he poured boiling water, scalding to death his enemy Minos. Eréndira momentarily considers scalding her grandmother to death by pouring boiling water in a similar conduit to her bath. She desists in her intention when the seemingly prescient old woman suddenly calls her name:

> Entonces quitó del fuego la olla hirviente, la levantó
> con mucho trabajo hasta la altura de la canal, y ya iba
> a echar el agua mortífera en el conducto de la bañera
> cuando la abuela gritó en el interior de la carpa:
> —¡Eréndira!
> Fue como si la hubiera visto. La nieta asustada por
> el grito, se arrepintió en el instante final (150).

An additional connection with the Theseus story is suggested when Ulises kills the grandmother in her own bed. Theseus killed the monstrous Procustes by beheading him to make him fit in his own bed.

Ulises, then, represents the principle of freedom, both as an example in the external world of ideas and as a psychological force ambivalently present in every human heart. This is evident not only in his efforts to achieve his own independence and to help Eréndira escape but also in the mythological associations of his name and acts, revolving around the quest for freedom from archetypal monsters and tyrants.

The grandmother's enslavement and abuse of Eréndira clearly places her in the role of monster-minotaur who imprisons her granddaughter in a psychological and, symbolically, a cultural labyrinth from which escape becomes extremely difficult. At the same time, certain images further identify the grandmother with the mythical Minotaur. She resembles the Minotaur because of her enormous size and her whale-like appearance: "La abuela, desnuda y grande, parecía una hermosa ballena blanca en la alberca de mármol (97). Later, Ulises and Eréndira jokingly refer to her as "la ballena blanca" (136), and on another occasion, yet closer to her mythological identity, she is described as "un buey acostado" (124). Other images suggesting her identity with the mythological monster are references to her "respiración enorme" (102) and her "respiración descomunal" (135), appropriate to the Minotaur. The beast's sire was a beautiful white bull of marine origin which Poseidon, the Greek sea-god gave to Minos' wife, Pasiphae, who fell in love with the bull.[10] Despite the generational displacement and the transformation, it is probable that her description of the grandmother as a beautiful white whale from the sea is intended to evoke the beautiful white bull of mythological fame. Perceptively, McMurray sees the white whale as a symbol of evil reminiscent of Melville's Moby Dick (111). Even a quasi-illicit kinship exists between Ariadne and the Minotaur on the one hand, and Eréndira and her grandmother on the other: Ariadne is the mythological monster's stepsister and Eréndira is the grandmother's bastard granddaughter.

The literary and mythological intertexts in "Eréndira" contribute to a multifaceted exploration of the nature of the colonial relations between Spain and its American colonies. García Márquez's subordination of these elements to his own purposes results both in a demythification of conventional interpretations of the colonial relations and a universalization of the complementary psychologies of the colonizer and the colonized underlying—and perpetuating—colonialism.

In "Eréndira," the noble exploits of Amadis have degenerated into smuggling, an indication of the self-seeking and lawlessness at the heart of the colonial enterprise. Colonial Spain, symbolized by the grandmother, is a type of Celestina, who cruelly exploits her own flesh and blood, partly out of a sheer will-to-power, and partly out of a love of ease and luxury. Through the grandmother's actions and the circumstances of her life the reader is led to perceive the decadence of colonial Spain and the degradation of everyone involved in the colonial process: both master and servant. Colonial Spain's decadence is illustrated everywhere, but most vividly perhaps in the grandmother's fondness for navigating in the stagnant waters of the "ciénagas del pasado" (98) and the brilliant green blood that literally explodes from her mortal wounds (161). . . .

García Márquez's evocation of the Ariadne-Theseus myth, as indicated above, has multiple implications, but one of the most meaningful, in another mythological displacement, is the parallel between the cruel sacrifice Minos makes of the young men of Athens to the Minotaur and the grandmother's exploitation of Eréndira, symbolizing colonial exploitation. Both the original and García Márquez's monster is slain, but in "Eréndira" freedom is revealed to involve much more than freedom *from* tyranny; it also entails freedom *to* develop one's powers, whether individual or cultural. Psychologically, Eréndira's abandonment of Ulises is an overreaction to a protracted deprivation of freedom, resulting in a desire for absolute freedom. Culturally, her only model for the good life has been the grandmother's will-to-power and materialism. For these reasons, she flees with the vest of gold. Symbolically, the circumstances of her flight suggest the individualism, lack of solidarity, and self-seeking rooted primarily in the Spanish American countries' colonial experience, making the conquest of a constructive freedom with an affirmative content a dream difficult to realize. Theseus turned Athens into a prosperous, democratic state; Erendira—and the newly liberated Spanish America—fails, at least initially, to fulfill the promise of freedom. García Márquez's subtle parable is not a sterile exercise casting blame on the exploiters, but rather an exposure of the psychohistorical roots of the present Spanish American situation, the all too prevalent lack of solidarity so effectively dramatized in *Cien años*. The mythological elements serve both to distance the reader from the events of the story and to universalize the significance of the story's events.

Notes

1 To distinguish between the Two Amadises the grandmother calls her

husband Amadís el grande, giving him a sobriquet like that of Amadís de Gaula (125).

[2] The grandmother's inordinate pride in her former beauty suggests the chivalric ideal of feminine beauty. Repeating a lover's words in one of her nostalgic dreams, she says: "Le he dado mil veces la vuelta al mundo y he visto a todas las mujeres de todas las naciones, así que tengo autoridad para decirte que eres la más altiva y la más servicial, la más hermosa de la tierra" (153).

[3] The story contains only one direct reference to mines: "minas de talco" (149), in or near the desert.

[4] García Márquez states in Fernández-Braso's "conversación" that the title "alude a los pregones de la feria" (138).

[5] Psychologically, her somnambulism may be a means of avoiding awareness of the endless tasks she must perform.

[6] The suddenness of Eréndira's acquisition of autonomy is very similar to that of Angela Vicario's achievement of autonomy in *Crónica de una muerte anunciada*, when she observes her mother's childish vanity while she is trying on her new glasses in front of a mirror (121).

[7] The wind is mentioned directly or indirectly (through storms) 27 times in the story.

[8] Palencia-Roth views the grandmother as a monster-minotaur and as "La Madre Terrible" (156-57), "esa terrible y gigantesca anciana que domina por completo las vidas de los adolescentes; que simboliza simultáneamente la angustia de la iniciación sexual y el dominio absoluto de la matriarca en la familia; y su metamorfosis más terrible, el vacio de la muerte" (153-54). This seems to me to be a quite accurate description of the psychological and sociological implications of the relationship between the grandmother and Eréndira. Palencia-Roth's remarks are relatively brief and do not elaborate on the possible allusion to figures other than Ariadne in the Theseus-Ariadne myth.

[9] The grandmother's keeping of an ostrich, a flightless bird, reinforces the impression of her enmity to freedom (101-103).

[10] Interestingly, Daedalus built a wooden cow for the bull. Pasiphae concealed herself inside the cow, which the bull mounted.

Chapter 6

A Grammatical Pre-text in
El amor en los tiempos del cólera

The slow gestation of García Márquez's novels is due in part to the utmost care with which the Colombian writer crafts each sentence for the maximum yield. A consummate stylist, he strives for—and habitually achieves—as many effects as possible with a single stroke. In his cogent study of *Cien años*, Mario Vargas Llosa aptly termed his style *totalizador* ["all-encompassing"] (479-576). As studies by critics such as Graciela Maturo (17-36 *et passim*), Michael Palencia-Roth, and Antonia Benítez Rojo and Hilda O. Benítez have clearly shown, García Márquez's all-encompassing style is the product of an astonishingly well-stocked and fertile imagination, enabling him to re-enact ancient myths in modern settings. In addition, he has harnessed a wide range of grammatical constructions, stylistic devices, and literary techniques to achieve his various literary ends. My focus here is on one grammatical construction, or stylistic device, which, although it is present throughout his fiction, stands out in *El amor en los tiempos del cólera*, appearing more than ninety times in the novel, and often almost of paragraph length.[1] The construction is the type of correlative conjunction that conforms to the following pattern: "No sólo . . . sino (que) . . ." or "No . . . sino (que) . . .". In the first case, the narrator usually gives two or more reasons for an event, act, or attitude, and in the second, makes a negative statement followed by a positive assertion.

The correlative conjunction (a form of the coordinating conjunction) generally serves to join ideas, to deny, to compare and contrast, and to provide supplementary information. It serves to make statements more economical and integrated.

García Márquez's use of this construction exemplifies all these general functions. And as will become clear later, it can serve as a kind of grammatical pre-text in his fiction. But what is noteworthy in his frequent recourse to the construction are the various ways he exploits it to increase the complexity of his fictional world, as well as to entertain and enlighten his readers. Although this construction is a major and significant technique, especially noticeable in *El amor*, it is of course one of many devices the novelist employs to achieve his ends. At first glance, the frequency of the novelist's recourse to this device suggests a stylistic tic. But García Márquez's consciousness as a writer makes this hypothesis extremely unlikely. Moreover, an analysis of his use of these constructions yields, in my view, interesting insights not only into the means the novelist employs to achieve a wide variety of effects but also into the nature of his sensibility and his understanding of the psychology of reading and the process of apperception. As will become evident below, the use of this type of correlative conjunction also parallels the Cervantine technique of providing multiple perspectives and individualizing his characters and situations, as well as contributing to the theme of appearances versus reality.

The correlative-conjunction construction contributes a constant dramatic element to García Márquez's writing. An implicit expectation, be it commonsensical, conventional, stereotypical, or dogmatic, is denied confirmation, or total confirmation. In contradicting the reader's expectations, the narrator creates a conflict producing dramatic tension. At the same time, he creates a momentary suspense through the denial that something is true or wholly true, the full truth of which, nevertheless, is disclosed almost immediately. In many cases, there is an implicit or hypothetical reader who has these false or partially false expectations. The real reader may or may not have such expectations, but can hardly avoid being affected by this stylistic device because of the dramatic tension it produces. In other cases, the expectations that are denied or altered are those of the characters themselves or those of society in general. These real and invented presuppositions constitute pre-texts on which the novelist feeds to create interest in what he writes (see Culler 114-18). When the Archbishop observes at a certain luncheon that those present are making history because liberals and conservatives, former enemies, are peacefully sitting at the same table, Juvenal Urbino, the host, resists the temptation to correct him:

> Sin embargo, no quiso contrariar al arzobispo. Aunque le
> habría gustado señalarle que nadie estaba en aquel
> almuerzo por lo que pensaba sino por los méritos de su
> alcurnia, y ésta había estado siempre por encima de los
> azares de la política y los honores de la guerra. Visto
> así, en efecto, no faltaba nadie (54).

With a single stroke the narrator dramatically refutes a superfi-
cial, clichéd way of thinking and throws in relief the hierarchical
and closed nature of the society.

When Fermina Daza returns to her former home after a
long stay with relatives in another province, the narrator ap-
prises the reader of the dramatic change effected in her personality: "Fermina Daza no era ya la hija única, a la vez consentida y
tiranizada por el padre, sino la dueña y señora de un imperio de
polvo y telarañas que sólo podía ser rescatado por la fuerza de un
amor invencible" (132). In the description of Fermina's reaction
to Paris, where she and Juvenal spent their honeymoon, the
narrator stresses the importance of a subjective or psychological
factor in her admiration of the city's beauty, slyly demystifying
its mythical attractiveness and beauty:

> A París, a pesar de su lluvia perpetua, de sus tenderos
> sórdidos y la grosería homérica de sus cocheros, había
> de recordarla siempre como la ciudad más hermosa del
> mundo, no porque en realidad lo fuera o no lo fuera, sino
> porque se quedó vinculada a la nostalgia de sus años más
> felices (277).

The dramatic elements of the correlative-conjunction construction such as surprise, the denial of expectations, the affirmation
of the unexpected, and comparisons and contrasts are designed
both to capture the reader's attention and facilitate his recall of
the situation described. The construction is designed *par excellence* to exploit sound principles of the psychology of learning.
Passing from the known and anticipated to the unknown and
unanticipated, García Márquez creates varying degrees of tension, which invariably increases suspense in anticipation of the
statement disclosing the full truth of the matter (Leahey and
Harris 108-09). It is true, of course, that a reader always feels a
certain tension until he finishes the reading of any sentence, but
the correlative conjunction-construction is designed to maxi-
mize the tension because it encompasses a denial followed by an
affirmation. In general, this construction corresponds to Gestalt

psychology's principle of closure: the urge human beings feel to complete or round off an incomplete perception (Leahey and Harris 113-14). The element of surprise and the comparisons and contrasts also correspond to well-known principles of the psychology of learning and apperception. The presence of these elements in a sentence both heighten readers' awareness and make a deeper, more lasting impression facilitating recall.

In varying degrees, every case of the use of the construction exhibits these principles. It is simply one significant aspect of García Márquez's mastery of what Ricardo Gullón aptly called "el olvidado arte de contar." I offer just a couple of interesting examples among the many appearing in the novel. When the church bell tolls for Juvenal Urbino's death, Florentino Ariza's reaction differs from what he—and the reader—might have expected:

> Todo lo que Florentino Ariza había hecho desde que Fermina Daza se casó, estaba fundado en la esperanza de esta noticia. Sin embargo, llegada la hora, no se sintió sacudido por la conmoción de triunfo que tantas veces había previsto en sus insomnios, sino por un zarpazo de terror: la lucidez fantástica de que lo mismo habría podido ser por él por quien tocaran a muerto (360).

Recently widowed, Fermina recalls with a new understanding her husband's reply (his "sapiencia insoportable") to her complaint that she was unhappy:

> "Recuerda siempre que lo más importante de un buen matrimonio no es la felicidad sino la estabilidad." Desde sus primeras soledades de viuda ella entendió que aquella frase no escondía la amenaza mezquina que le había atribuido en su tiempo, sino la piedra lunar que les había proporcionado a ambos tantas horas felices (390).

Because it approaches a situation or the motivation of a character from unsuspected angles, inhibiting an automatic response, this construction frequently lends itself to what the Russian formalist Shklovsky called "defamiliarization" (11-24). Such defamiliarization militates against stereotypical perceptions and ideas, and also serves to capture the reader's attention because of the freshness of the perspective. In the following passage the narrator describes Fermina's reaction to the various signs of Juvenal Urbino's aging in a manner that associates diverse stages of human life often compared in describing the effects of old age, but with nuances of difference here producing a fresh perspective:

> Ella había ido descubriendo poco a poco la incertidumbre de los pasos de su marido, sus trastornos de humor, las fisuras de su memoria, su costumbre reciente de sollozar dormido, pero no los identificó como los signos inequívocos del óxido final, sino como una vuelta feliz a la infancia. Por eso no lo trataba como a un anciano difícil sino como a un niño senil, y aquel engaño fue providencial para ambos porque los puso a salvo de la compasión (42).

Here, García Márquez avails himself of this stylistic device to describe Fermina's refusal to fall into a clichéd way of thinking and acting. Implicit in this situation is the Cervantine notion that if perceptions do not always create reality, they nearly always have real consequences.

A case of defamiliarization anticipating the subsequent intentional association between love and cholera is evident in the description of Florentino's symptoms of illness while awaiting a reply to his first love letter to Fermina:

> Pero cuando empezó a esperar la respuesta a su primera carta, la ansiedad se le complicó con cagatines y vómitos verdes, perdió el sentido de la orientación y sufría desmayos repentinos, y su madre se aterrorizó porque su estado no se parecía a los desórdenes del amor sino a los estragos del cólera (86).

The multiple perspectives made possible through the correlative-conjunction construction enable García Márquez to create a more complex fictional reality and, specifically, a superior psychological realism. If what literature (specifically poetry) does best, as Aristotle affirmed, is express the universal through the concrete, the construction performs this function extraordinarily well. It is especially apt for individualizing human affairs and the characters' motivation; wary of facile explanations, through it García Márquez achieves a deeper penetration into the mysteries of human conduct. This stylistic device enables the novelist to create with utmost economy what E. M.

Forster termed "round" and "dynamic" characters, characters that possess multiple traits and are capable of surprising us convincingly in the display of unsuspected traits in new situations (67-78).

Shortly after the suicide of his friend Jeremiah de Saint Amour, Juvenal learns that his friend had concealed from him certain unflattering matters in his past and the fact that he had a mistress. Fermina is surprised at her husband's anger and disillusionment:

> Ella suponía que su esposo no apreciaba a Jeremiah de Saint-Amour por lo que había sido antes, sino por lo que empezó a ser desde que llegó sin más prendas encima que su mochila de exiliado, y no podía entender por qué lo consternaba de aquel modo la revelación tardía de su identidad (49-50).

When Fermina points out that having a mistress is typical of men like Jeremiah, her husband rejoins that she simply does not understand how he feels: "No entiendes nada—dijo—. Lo que me indigna no es lo que fue ni lo que hizo, sino el engaño en que nos mantuvo a todos durante tantos años" (50). Learning of the concealment simply provokes the rebellion of Juvenal's pride.

Florentino's reaction upon seeing Fermina pregnant may be unexpected, because it is atypical, but nonetheless it rings true psychologically in his case because he is intropunitive: "Florentino no sintió celos ni rabia, sino un gran desprecio de sí mismo. Se sintió pobre, feo, inferior, y no sólo indigno de ella sino de cualquier otra mujer sobre la tierra" (202).

In several cases a character's conduct is overdetermined, though one of the causes of the act may be established as dominant. This is the case in Florentino's gradual abandonment of his habit of accompanying women to a local hotel to make love:

> Pero después ya no pudo decir si su costumbre de fornicar sin esperanzas era una necesidad de la conciencia o un simple vicio del cuerpo. Iba cada vez menos al hotel de paso, no sólo porque sus intereses andaban por otros rumbos, sino porque no le gustaba que lo vieran allí en andanzas distintas de las muy domésticas y castas que ya le conocían (229).

Eliminating several possible reasons for Fermina's deci-

sion to accept Juvenal's marriage proposal, the narrator gives
very personal motives for her affirmative decision, revealing
that she accepts his proposal out of fear of being left out of the
lottery of marriage rather than because of the attractiveness of
the match:

> Pero lo hizo, en el minuto crucial de su vida, sin tomar
> en cuenta para nada la belleza viril del pretendiente,
> ni su riqueza legendaria, ni su gloria temprana, ni
> ninguno de sus tantos méritos reales, sino aturdida por el
> miedo de la oportunidad que se le iba y la inminencia de
> los veintiún años, que era su límite confidencial para
> rendirse al destino (269).

Underlying the motives for her decision lurk social expectations
she has assimilated. If a strong-willed person such as Fermina
Daza marries on account of such fears, one could hardly expect
less independent young women to resist the temptation.

One of literature's perennial tasks is to destroy outworn
myths or texts and replace or revitalize them with new ones. As
numerous critics have pointed out, García Márquez's fiction is
incessantly devoted to this task. Mythological allusions and parallels and other intertexts abound in his stories and novels,
never in slavish imitation of the original but rather disguised,
adapted, and transformed to suit his own purposes. The correlative-conjunction construction affords him the opportunity on a
smaller scale to demythologize, or at least demystify, throughout
El amor a variety of myths and texts. Consequently, a thread of
demythologization, or demystification, visibly runs throughout
the novel, reinforcing the impression of a demythologizing effort with regard to the nature of love on the whole as well as in
the details. The correlative-conjunction construction consists of
a denial or a modification of conventional expectations, dogmas,
unexamined assumptions, and unquestioned beliefs, virtually
constituting on a minor scale myths or prior texts (pre-texts) that
the novelist wishes to destroy or, at least, alter. In a single sentence he is able to state both the "myth" or "text" to be wholly or
partially destroyed and replace it with a new myth or text, adequate to the circumstances. An interesting example of demythologization on a minor scale is evident in the passage cited
above, regarding the Archbishop's observation about liberals and
conservatives sitting at the same table. The myth destroyed is
that the fundamental condition for social intercourse among the

city's aristocrats is political homogeneity when in fact the fundamental condition for such intercourse is a distinguished lineage. In another passage cited earlier, we find a demythologization of the reputation Paris enjoys as the most beautiful city in the world. I refer to the passage describing Fermina's opinion that Paris is the most beautiful city in the world because she associates the city with the happiest years of her youth. In view of Paris's disadvantages, enumerated at the beginning of the sentence, Fermina's recollection of its beauty seems quite paradoxical, but it is comprehensible viewed from the vantage point of her nostalgia.

Fermina's reaction to Juvenal's confession to a priest of his illicit love affair casts doubt on the legitimacy of the confessional, especially when the confession violates the privacy of another person. Prior to the description of Fermina's reaction, the reader is informed that "desde el colegio tenía la convicción de que la gente de iglesia carecía de cualquier virtud inspirada por Dios" (327). We are also told that this had been a cause of discord between Juvenal and her, but a discord which they had learned to manage. Fermina is upset by this invasion of what she considers her private life:

> Pero que su esposo le hubiera permitido al confesor inmiscuirse hasta ese punto en una intimidad que no era sólo la suya, sino también la de ella, era algo que iba más allá de todo (327).

In a novel which destroys the myths about the capacity of the elderly for passionate love, it should come as no surprise that along the way the novelist would seek to demolish other myths about the elderly. Florentino's almost centenarian uncle, León XII, opposes relinquishing the steamship's monopoly or the river because to do so would seem to him a trashing of all his previous victories against opponents of the monopoly rather than because at his age he is lacking in imagination or vision, as most people thought:

> La tozudez del viejo les parecía natural, no porque la vejez lo hubiera vuelto menos visionario de lo que fue siempre, como solía decirse con demasiada facilidad, sino porque la renuncia al monopolio debía parecerle como botar en la basura los trofeos de una batalla histórica que él y sus hermanos habían librado solos en los tiempos heroicos contra adversarios poderosos del mundo entero (349).

Notwithstanding the substantial differences between *el amor* and *Don Quixote*, there are also striking parallels between the two novels that are strongly reinforced by use of the correlative-conjunction construction. Both Florentino and Don Quixote are consumed by a passion for an idealized lady; both pursue the ideal with fanaticism. Don Quixote is inspired by nostalgia for a nonexistent past, and Florentino is inspired by nostalgia for a past amorous relation that was more illusion than reality—an unrequited love. Both heroes find inspiration and guidance in romantic literature: Don Quixote in chivalric books, Florentino in sentimental poetry of the past and the present, which he commits to memory:

> No sólo tenía una memoria asombrosa para los versos
> sentimentales de su tiempo, cuyas novedades se vendían
> en folletos callejeros de a dos centavos, sino que clavaba
> con alfileres en las paredes los poemas que más le gusta-
> ban, para leerlos de viva voz a cualquier hora (260).

With heroic singlemindedness both characters devote their lives to a woman, whom they idealize in varying degrees. The narrator writes of Florentino's "ambición de amor que ninguna contrariedad de este mundo ni del otro lograría quebrantar" (219). A notable difference between the two characters is that Cervantes's hero sublimates his passion for Dulcinea, but Florentino manages to enjoy numerous love affairs without relinquishing his goal of winning Fermina's love. Don Quixote and Florentino are both individualists, ever disposed to pursuing their own goals in defiance of conventional values. Don Quixote acts openly and often rashly; Florentino employs a combination of prudence and practical psychology.

The Cervantine influence or spirit reveals its presence through *El amor* especially through the correlative-conjunction construction. This construction is particularly apt for developing the theme of appearances vs. reality, for creating multiple perspectives, and for individualizing characters and events, all of which are *par excellence* characteristic of Cervantine realism. Although virtually every instance of the use of this stylistic device exemplifies these characteristics, I choose, for illustration however, only a few of the more interesting examples. In a statement revealing the reality behind the appearances of piety, the narrator discloses the superstitious nature of the pilgrims who swarm to the city ostensibly to hear the sermons preached by the Bishop of Ríohacha:

> Detrás vinieron peregrinos de comarcas remotas,
> músicos de acordeones, vendedores ambulantes de comi-
> das y amuletos, y la hacienda estuvo tres días desbor-
> dada de invalidos y desahuciados, que en realidad no
> venían por los sermones doctos y las indulgencias ple-
> narias, sino por los favores de la mula, de la cual se
> decía que hacía milagros a escondidas del dueño (309).

Although Andrea Varón's sexual improprieties are public knowledge, no one has come forth with concrete proof of them, not out of a desire to protect her but rather because her distinguished lovers have much more to lose than she if there is a scandal. Hence, a profit-and-loss analysis yields a different perspective on the situation.

> Repartió sus dádivas de placer hasta donde le alcanzó
> el cuerpo, y aunque su conducta impropia era de dominio
> público, nadie hubiera podido exhibir contra ella una
> prueba terminante, proque sus cómplices insignes la pro-
> tegieron tanto como a sus propias vidas, conscientes de
> que no era ella sino ellos los que tenían más que perder
> con el escándalo (15).

Florentino is said to climb stairs more slowly with the passing of years not because it is physically more demanding but rather for another less obvious reason, having to do with his particular perspective.

> A medida que pasaban los años demoraba más para
> subir, no porque le costara más trabajo, como él se
> apresuraba a explicar, sino porque cada vez subía con
> más cuidado (406-07).

When Florentino, many years after Fermina has married Juvenal, begins walking in the vicinity of her house, he does so for a reason that is not immediately obvious; but which by presenting an unsuspected motive individualizes his psychology:

> Volvió a rondar la quinta de Fermina Daza con las
> mismas ansias con que lo hacía tantos años antes en el
> parquecito de Los Evangelios, pero no con la intención
> calculada de que ella lo viera, sino con la única de verla
> para saber que continuaba en el mundo (301).

In summary, the correlative-conjunction construction is a

frequently-used and major stylistic device in García Márquez's *El amor*. His ability to harness a single construction with such imagination and economy to achieve so wide a range of effects is a measure of his self-consciousness as a stylist and writer. Given García Márquez's self-consciousness as a writer, the details, as well as the general patterns of his style, manifestly offer a rich field for further exploration.

Note

[1] Proving García Márquez's preference for this type of construction in this novel *vis-à-vis* his other writings and those of other writers would be a difficult, if not impossible, task. I was certainly struck during my first reading of the novel by the frequent appearance of the construction. As far as the relative frequency is concerned, I rely wholly on a straightforward count and the intersubjective "confirmation" of other readers for a validation of my claim. Be that as it may, the issue of validating the relative frequency of the appearance of the construction is separate from that of the uses García Márquez makes of the construction.

Conclusion

Given the similarities between the cultural milieu of García Lorca's Spain and that of García Márquez's Colombia, as well as the broad ideological affinities shared by the two writers, it comes as no surprise to find echoes of the playwright's *La casa de Bernarda Alba* in the novelist's work. After all, *Bernarda Alba* is Lorca's most widely read and widely staged play. Most educated Hispanics are familiar with the play, and though he never mentions Lorca as a writer who has influenced him, it is evident that García Márquez is thoroughly familiar with this powerful play and that he borrowed from it both in *La mala hora* and in *Cien años de soledad*. In general, both writers seek to vindicate the claims of instinctual life against the repressive morality of an ultraconservative Catholicism. *La mala hora* reveals not only similar thematic concerns but also a use of imagery and symbolism reminiscent of *Bernarda Alba*. Moreover, as our analysis has shown, in both *La mala hora* and *Cien años*, García Márquez has appropriated specific incidents from the play for his own uses. Characters in *Cien años* such as Fernanda, Amaranta, and, in certain moments, Ursula are created very much in the mold of Bernarda Alba. A comparison of the manner in which the two writers present similar incidents, reveals that in *Cien años*, however, in keeping with the carnivalization of his discourse, García Márquez includes a strong dosage of humor that is missing in Lorca's play.

As odd as it may seem, much of García Márquez's magical realism, especially the "inventions" and "discoveries" in *Cien años*, "presupposes," to use Culler's word, the philosophy of pragmatism. The element of pragmatism is integrated into his writing in such a fashion as to lend credibility to what is being claimed at the same time that it creates in the reader a sense of *lo real maravilloso,* a sense of the miraculousness of all reality. García Márquez has often said that everything he writes has a basis in reality. The presence of a pragmatic element even in his magical-realist style lends credence to his claim.

The Colombian writer's admiration of Faulkner is well known, and the Mississippi writer's influence on his fiction is well documented. However, the similarities between Eula Varner in *The Hamlet* and Remedios, la bella, in *Cien años* have been overlooked. Although there are important differences, the resemblances between the two characters in general and in some of the details are too close to be accidental. The comparative analysis of these two characters further suggested that García Márquez may have learned something about techniques of exaggeration from Faulkner. Another affinity that became evident in the analysis is both novelists' frequent recourse to the coordinate-conjunction construction: "not . . . but . . .," of which more later.

Critics have commented on the Rabelaisian flavor of *Cien años* since its appearance in 1967. However, there have been few studies of this novel and his other fiction within the framework of Bakhtin's theory and history of the carnivalesque tradition. Based on Bakhtin's theory, the analysis of *Cien años* and *Crónica* has shown how García Márquez assimilates that tradition for his own purposes. Both Rabelais and García Márquez avail themselves of carnivalesque elements to undermine certain aspects of what Bakhtin calls "official culture" or the "official version," whether this be social, economic, political, religious, or aesthetic. In *Cien años,* the novelist restores laughter to a tradition which, according to Bakhtin, under the influence of romanticism had become devoid of humor.

What had not been noticed until recently (by Isabel Rodríguez-Vergara) is that carnivalized discourse in García Márquez's fiction is not limited to works like *Cien años,* with its hyperbolic style and larger-than-life characters and events, but it is also present in *Crónica,* albeit in a more subtle form. Although this novel rarely provokes the laughter that *Cien años* does, it, too, in a subtle and almost imperceptible fashion militates against "official culture," especially religious dogma and the townspeople's assimilation of that dogma in their lives. In both novels, the primacy of the body is implicitly extolled *a la* Rabelais against the repression of the instinctual life sanctioned by the Church. Through the carnivalization of his discourse,

García Márquez attempts to correct the onesided ideal of human conduct promoted by ultraconservative Catholicism.

T. S. Eliot once expressed an opinion to the effect that a writer should write with a knowledge of all Western literature in his bones, from Homer on down to the present. García Márquez certainly complies with Eliot's dictum in starting with Homer, though this is less well known than is his admiration, for example, of Sophocles's plays, or his knowledge of Greek and Roman mythology. The study of *Crónica* has disclosed that certain aspects of the violence of this novel hark back to the *Iliad*. Moreover, in *Crónica* there occurs a degradation of the original myths contained in the ancient epic. The wielders of the arms in *Crónica* are no longer noble heroes but rather ignorant hog butchers. The arms themselves, the elegant swords, sometimes fashioned by the gods themselves in the *Iliad*, are transformed in *Crónica* into crude, rusty knives once used for butchering hogs. The Vicario twins are unconscious instruments of the townspeople's more or less unconscious collective will just as the *Iliad*'s characters are tools of the gods.

The analysis of "Eréndira" provides an additional illustration of the novelist's assimilation of Greek myths. In this case he avails himself of Greek mythology to explore the theme of colonialism in Latin America. At the same time the integration into his exploration of fragments of Greek mythology universalizes his treatment of the dynamics of colonialism. Evident in the analysis of this story was a strong penchant for displacement of the names of the characters from whom or what they represented. The numerous and diverse intertexts made this story a challenging jigsaw puzzle.

García Márquez's frequent recourse to the coordinate-conjunction construction in *El amor en los tiempos del cólera* serves to increase interest and suspense in a very economical way, but it also constitutes a kind of internal pre-text on which the novelist feeds. The construction often creates a presupposition on the reader's part which the narrator then denies or attenuates in some way. As indicated above, this is a construction which also appears frequently in Faulkner's *The Hamlet*.

García Márquez's numerous and varied intertexts create a multiplicity of voices in his fiction, a maximum number of perspectives, which he achieves with the utmost unobtrusiveness and subtlety. The boldness with which he disguises his intertexts through displacement, condensation, and other devices is

breathtaking, but this very boldness makes the reader's collaboration, the process of deconstructing and reconstructing, all the
more challenging and, when successful, exhilarating. Although
such disguises permit the novelist modestly to conceal his cre-
ative processes and to reduce whatever "anxiety of influence" he
may feel, they also serve to enrich the text and the reader's experience of the text.

Works Cited

Anderson, Reed. *Federico García Lorca*. New York: Grove, 1984.

Andrigueto, Dulce. "El falso poder de la autoridad en *La mala hora*." *En el punto de mira: Gabriel García Márquez*. Ed. Ana María Hernández. Madrid: Pliegos, 1985: 23-29.

Arendt, Hannah. *Eichmann in Jerusalem: A Report on the Banality of Evil*. New York: Viking, 1963.

Arnau, Carmen. *El mundo mítico de Gabriel García Márquez*. Barcelona: Peninsula, 1975.

Bakhtin, Mikhail. *The Dialogic Imagination*. Trans. Caryl Emerson and Michael Holquist. Ed. Michael Holquist. Austin: U of Texas P, 1981.

—. *Problems of Dostoevsky's Poetics*. Trans. R. W. Rotsel, Ann Arbors Ardis, 1973.

—. *Rabelais and His World*. Trans. Hélène Iswolksy. Bloomington: Indiana UP, 1984.

Barthes, Roland. *The Pleasure of the Text*. Trans. Richard Miller. New York: Hill and Wang, 1975.

Bell-Villada, Gene. *García Marquez: The Man and His Work*. Chapel Hill & London: U of North Carolina P, 1990.

Benitez Rojo, Antonio and Hilda O. Benítez. "Eréndira liberada: la subversión del mito del macho occidental." *Revista Iberoamericana*. 50 (1984): 1057-75.

Borges, Jorge Luis. "Funes el memorioso." *Obras completas: 1923-1972*. Buenos Aires: Emecé, 1974.

Crispin, John. "*La casa de Bernarda Alba* dentro de la visión mítica lorquiana." In *La casa de Bernarda Alba*. Ed. Ricardo Doménech. Madrid: Cátedra, 1985: 171-85.

Culler, Jonathan. *The Pursuit of Signs: Semiotics, Literature, Deconstruction*. Ithaca, NY: Cornell UP, 1981.

Delay, Florence and Jacqueline de Labriolle. "Márquez est-il le

Faulkner colombien?" *Revue de Littérature Comparée* 47 (1973): 88-123.

Doménech, Ricardo. Símbolo, mito y rito en *La casa de Bernarda Alba*." *La Casa de Bernarda Alba*. Ed. Ricardo Doménech. Madrid: Catédra, 1985: 187-208.

Eagleton, Terry. *Literary Theory: An Introduction*. Minneapolis: U of Minnesota P, 1983.

Faulkner, William. *The Hamlet*. New York: Random House, 1964.

Fernández-Braso, Miguel. *La soledad de Gabriel García Márquez: una conversación infinita*. Barcelona: Planeta, 1982.

Forster, E. M. *Aspects of the Novel*. San Diego: Harcourt Brace Jovanovich, 1985.

García Lorca, Federico. *La casa de Bernarda Alba. La zapatera prodigiosa*. 11th ed. Madrid: Espasa-Calpe, 1987.

García Márquez, Gabriel. *Cien años de soledad*. Buenos Aires: Sudamericana, 1969.

—. *Crónica de una muerte anunciada*. Bogotá: La Oveja Negra, 1981.

—. *El olor de la guayaba: conversaciones con Plinio Apuleyo Mendoza*. Barcelona: Bruguera, 1982.

—. "Un señor muy viejo con unas alas enormes." *La incréible y triste historia de la cándida Eréndira y de su abuela desalmada*. Barcelona: Barral, 1977.

—. "El ahogado más hermoso del mundo." *La incréible y triste historia de la cándida Eréndira y de su abuela desalmada*. Barcelona: Barral, 1977.

—. "La increíble y triste historia de la cándida Eréndira y de su abuela desalmada." *La increíble y triste historia de la cándida Eréndira y de su abuela desalmada*. Barcelona: Barral, 1977.

—. *El amor en los tiempos del colera*. 3rd ed. Buenos Aires: Editorial Sudamericana, 1986.

—. *El coronel no tiene quien le escriba*. Buenos Aires, Editorial Sudamericana, 1973.

—. *El general en su laberinto*. Buenos Aires: Editorial Sudamericana, 1989.

—. *La mala hora*. Buenos Aires, Editorial Sudamericana, 1976.

—. *El otoño del patriarca*. Barcelona: Playa & Janes, 1975.

—. "The Solitude of America (Nobel Lecture, 1982). *Gabriel García Márquez and the Powers of Fiction*. Ed. Julio Ortega. Austin: U of Texas P, 1988.

Gullón, Ricardo.   Garcia Márquez: *El olvidado arte de contar*.
Madrid: Taurus, 1970.

Hamilton, Edith. *Mythology*. Boston: Little, Brown and Co.,
1942.

Harss, Luis. *Los nuestros*. Buenos Aires: Editorial Sudamericana, 1977.

Hazera, Lydia D. "Estructura y temática de *La mala hora* de
Gabriel García Márquez." *Thesaurus* 28 (1973): 471-81.

Higginbottom, Virginia. The Comic Spirit of *Federico García
Lorca*. Austin and London: U of Texas P, 1976.

Homer. *The Iliad*. Trans. Samuel Butler. Roslyn, NY: Walter J.
Black, 1942.

James, William. *Pragmatism*. New York: Meridian, 1955.

Kirsner, Robert. "Four Colombian Novels of Violence." *Hispania* 16 (March 1966): 70-74.

Kristeva, Julia. *Desire in Language: A Semiotic Approach to
Language and Art*. Trans. Thomas Gora & Alice Jardine.
New York: Columbia UP, 1980.

—. *The Kristeva Reader*. Ed. Toril Moi. New York: Columbia
UP, 1986.

—. *Revelation in Poetic Language*. Trans. Margaret Waller.
New York: Columbia UP, 1984.

Kuhn, Thomas. *The Structure of Scientific Revolutions*.
Chicago: U of Chicago P, 1969.

Kulin, Katalin. *Creación mítica en la obra de García Márquez*.
Budapest: Akadémiai Kiadó, 1980.

Leahey, Thomas Hardy and Richard Jackson Harris. *Human
Learning*. Englewood Cliffs, NJ: Prentice Hall, 1985.

Londré, Felicia Hardison. *Federico García Lorca*. New York: Un-
gar, 1984.

Luchting, Wolfgang A. "Lampooning Literature: *La mala hora*."
Critical Essays on Gabriel García Márquez. Ed. George R.
McMurray. Boston: G. G. Hall, 1987.

McGrady, Donald. "Acerca de una colección desconocida de re-
latos de Gabriel García Márquez." *Thesaurus* 27 (1972):
293-320.

McMurray, George R. *Gabriel García Márquez*. New York: Un-
gar, 1977.

Mallet, Brian. "García Márquez and François Rabelais: un
análisis del cuento, 'Los funerales de la Mamá Grande.'"
Revista de la Universidad de Antioquía 184 (enero-mayo
de 1972): 25-41.

Maturo, Graciela. *Claves simbólicas de García Márquez.* Buenos Aires: F. García Cambeiro, 1972.

Minta, Stephen, *García Márquez: Writer of Colombia.* New York: Harper & Row, 1987.

Morellia, Gabriela. "A coloquio con Gabriel García Márquez." *Studi di Letteratura Ispano-americana* 5 (1974): 121-30.

Nietzsche, Friedrich. "Beyond Good and Evil." *The Philosophy of Nietzsche.* New York: Modern Library, 1937.

Palencia-Roth, Michael. *Gabriel García Márquez: la línea, el círculo y las metamorfosis del mito.* Madrid: Gredos, 1983.

—. "Prisms of Consciousness: The New Worlds of Columbus and García Márquez." *Critical Perspectives on Gabriel García Márquez.* Ed. Bradley A. Shaw and Nora Godwin. Lincoln, NB: Society of Spanish and Spanish American Studies, 1986.

—. "Intertextualities: Three Metamorphoses of Myths in *The Autumn of the Patriarch.*" *Gabriel García Márquez and the Powers of Fiction.* Ed. Julio Ortega. Austin: U of Texas P, 1988. 34-60.

Oberhelman, Harley D. *The Presence of Faulkner in the Writings of García Márquez.* Lubbock: Texas Tech UP, 1980.

Parisier Plottel, Jeanine, and Hanna Chaney, Eds. *Intertextuality: New Perspectives in Criticism.* Vol. 2. New York: New York Literary Forum, 1978.

Penuel, Arnold M. "Death and the Maiden: The Demythologization of Virginity in García Márquez's *Cien años de soledad.*" *Hispania* 66 (Dec. 1983): 552-60.

—. "The Sleep of Vital Reason in García Márquez's *Crónica de una muerte anunciada.*" *Hispania* 68 (Dec. 1985): 753-66.

Pérez Galdós, Benito. *Obras completas.* Vol. 4. 3rd ed. Ed. Federico Carlos Sainz de Robles. Madrid: Aguilar, 1954.

Pope, Randolph D. "Transparency and Illusion in *Chronicle of a Death Foretold.*" *Latin American Literary Review* 15 (Jan. -June 1987): 183-200.

Rabelais, François. *Gargantua and Pantagruel.* Trans. Barton Raffel. New York and London: Norton, 1990.

Rodríguez-Vergara, Isabel. *El mundo satírico de Gabriel García Márquez.* Madrid: Pliegos, 1991.

Rama, Angel. "Un novelista de la violencia americana." *Gabriel García Márquez.* Ed. Peter G. Earle. Madrid: Taurus, 1981. 30-39.

Rorty, Richard. *Consequences of Pragmatism*. Minneapolis: U of Minnesota P, 1982.

—. *Contingency, Irony, and Solidarity*. New York: Cambridge UP, 1989.

Rosenblatt, Angel. Presentación. *Amadis de Gaula*. Buenos Aires: Losada, 1963.

Ruiz Ramón, Francisco. *Historia del teatro espanol: siglo XX*. Madrid: Cátedra, 1975.

Shklovsky, Victor. "Art as Technique." *Russian Formalist Criticism: Four Essays*. Ed. Lee T. Lemon and Marion J. Reis. Lincoln: U of Nebraska P, 1965.

Sims, Robert L. "Periodismo, ficción, espacio carnavelesco y oposiciones binarias: la creación de la infraestructura novelística de Gabriel García Márquez." *Hispania* 71 (March 1988): 50-60.

Snell, Susan. "William Faulkner, un guía sureño a la ficción de Garcia Márquez." *En el punto de mira: Gabriel García Márquez*. Ed. Ana Maria Hernández de López. Madrid: Editorial Pliegos, 1985: 315-326.

Torres, Benjamín. *Gabriel García Márquez o la alquimia del incesto*. Madrid: Playor, 1987.

Turner, Harriet S. "Circularity and Closure in Lorca's Trilogy." *The World of Nature in the Works of Federico García Lorca*. Ed. Joseph W. Zdenek. Rock Hill, SC: Winthrop Studies on Major Modern Writers, 1980: 101-15.

Vargas Llosa, Mario. *A Writer's Reality*. Ed. Myron I. Lichtblau. Syracuse: Syracuse UP, 1991.

—. *Historia de un deicidio*. Caracas: Monte Avila, 1971.

Weingarten, Barry E. "Nature as Unnatural." In *The World of Nature in the Works of Federico García Lorca*. Ed. Joseph W. Zdenek. Rock Hill, SC: Winthrop Studies on Major Modern Writers, 1980: 129-38.

Williams, Raymond. *Gabriel García Marquez*. Boston: Twayne, 1984.

Wood, Michael. *Gabriel García Márquez: "One Hundred Years of Solitude."* Cambridge: Cambridge UP, 1990.